HOW TO MAKE A FORTUNE

ON AIRBNB

TIM VERNOOIJ

Any mentioned trademarks, service marks, product names, and features are property of their respective owners and are only used for reference.

Book website: www.rentalsmarketing.com/book

First edition: February 2021

ISBN: 978-84-09-22300-8

Contents

Preface

Some opportunities only come once in a lifetime, and this truly felt like one. November 28, 2014. It was an early morning in the Aruba Marriott Resort & Stellaris Casino. The sun was out, and the sky was blue - it looked like it would be another beautiful sunny Caribbean day on this laidback island. I traveled to Aruba often, unfortunately not for holidays. I was in Aruba for one of my quarterly business trips to meet with hotel and property management company executives.

I worked for Booking.com as an account manager and vacation rental specialist for the Caribbean region, based in Santo Domingo, the Dominican Republic. Due to my Dutch origin, I was responsible for the performance of all properties listed on Booking.com in the Dutch Caribbean Islands: Aruba, Bonaire, Curacao, St. Maarten, St. Eustatius, and Saba. And as a vacation rental specialist for the Caribbean, I focused on getting the largest Caribbean property management companies on board and optimized their performance. Certainly not a bad job for a 26-year-old travel enthusiast, getting paid to travel around the Caribbean while staying in fancy hotels and villas. However, just like many things in life, things became routine faster than I thought. After two and a half years, even a job like this started feeling like a "real" job. So I started looking for a new challenge.

Back to Aruba. It was 7 AM. My alarm clock went off; I stepped out of bed, took a shower, got dressed, and opened my laptop to check my email and schedule for the day. I opened my inbox and scrolled through the emails. One new email, in particular, got my attention. The title said: "Should we be talking?" I assumed it would be some spam message and wanted to click it away until I realized it was a message from a LinkedIn recruiter in my LinkedIn inbox. I was quite surprised because I frequently received recruiter messages through LinkedIn, but not from LinkedIn itself. I quickly opened the message, which said: "Hi Tim, my name is Sean, and I work on the LinkedIn Recruitment Team in Dublin, Ireland. I am sure you get contacted quite regularly by recruiters on LinkedIn, but your profile caught my eye, which has led me to reach out to you! You seem to be very involved with the internet and hi-tech industries, which is exactly the space LinkedIn operates in. I'm sure you are relatively happy at Booking.com, but would you be interested in having a very open and casual chat with me?" I was quite surprised. It sounded interesting, so I decided to accept his offer for a chat. I replied to Sean: "Hi Sean, thank you for your message! I very much appreciate your interest in having a chat. I am happy at Booking.com, but I'm always open to hearing about opportunities when they present themselves. When is the best time to schedule a telephone call over the next week?"

A couple of days later, Sean and I had the call. Sean offered me to become part of the LinkedIn Sales Solutions team in the European LinkedIn head office in Dublin, Ireland. I have always wanted to start my own business. However, I agreed to myself that my time to learn as much as possible before starting my own business would be in my twenties during my first few years of working experience. And I thought that working for LinkedIn would be an excellent opportunity for me to learn more about sales while working for another great technology company. But not only that, the benefits would be fantastic too.

However, there were a couple of reasons, which made me hesitate. First, I didn't know much about Ireland, just that it isn't known for having the best climate on earth. Second, my spouse Jennifer and I recently acquired our first home, a beautiful modern two-bedroom apartment in the city center of Santo Domingo. At that time, the apartment still was under construction, and it would only take a couple of months to finish. The idea of moving to another country without being able to live inside our brand-new home felt strange. Third, due to her Dominican Nationality, Jennifer couldn't just move to Ireland; it would take months to get the paperwork done.

In the end, however, we concluded that we were ready for a new challenge and decided to go for it; we knew we could always come back if things wouldn't turn out well. A couple of weeks - and five job interviews later, I got hired at LinkedIn. They would arrange Jennifer's visa, and we decided to rent out our new apartment in Santo Domingo and pack our suitcases for a new adventure in Ireland.

In March 2015, we received the key to our newly constructed apartment in Santo Domingo. I had already moved to Ireland, and

Jennifer was waiting in the Dominican Republic for her Irish Visa. Jennifer took advantage of her time in the Dominican Republic and furnished the apartment with our used furniture. We were hoping that renting a furnished apartment would allow us to increase our monthly rental income. Our idea was to rent it out fixed, but we were willing to try short-term renting if it would be profitable.

Once we decorated the apartment, we listed it on Booking.com. A couple of days passed by, but we didn't get any reservations. The listing profile was 100% completed, had good quality photos, a fair nightly rate, flexible restrictions, but nothing seemed to work. Jennifer said, "Maybe we should forget about renting the apartment as a short-term rental and try to find someone interested in renting it long-term." We were close to giving up at that point, but something told me to give it another try. I told her: "let's give it two more weeks. Let me publish the apartment on this growing booking platform for short-term rentals called' Airbnb.' Let's see if they can bring us any bookings." I created the listing on Airbnb, and luckily within 24 hours, we had our first booking. A 12-night stay × $100 per night = worth $1.200 in total. We were more than amazed. This apartment has a monthly value on the long-term rental market at around $1.000. With just one Airbnb booking of 12 nights, we generated more than what the apartment would generate in one month on the long-term rental market.

We started experimenting a bit with the rates and profile settings. We soon figured out that our best standard nightly rate was around $110 per night, resulting in average monthly occupancy of approximately 90% and average monthly earnings of about $3.000.

As I started my new full-time job at LinkedIn, we agreed that Jennifer would take over daily communication with guests, cleaners, and manage key handling. This way, I would only have to focus on keeping the profile, rates, and availability up to date, while automizing as much as possible.

This apartment is located in a modern residential tower where some family members and investors own properties too. Soon they figured out that we were offering our apartment with great success on Airbnb. They reached out and asked us if we would be interested in helping them rent their properties on Airbnb too. "Absolutely!" we said. Within three months after publishing our apartment, we were managing five other apartments within the same building on Airbnb.

We worked with the property owners in two different ways. We would either lease a property long-term, furnish it and then publish it on Airbnb - known as the rental arbitrage model - or work with the owners on a commission per reservation base, known as the property management model. Mostly, working on a commission per reservation base with property owners/investors turned out for us to be a very lucrative way of making money without any risk. It allowed us to obtain a decent income.

As time passed by, we decided to take every opportunity of adding additional properties to our portfolio. It was effortless to make money on Airbnb; it didn't matter what type of property we would publish or how it looked; they all got plenty of reservations. Within one year, we managed 16 properties. Business was so good that we decided to purchase a second investment property, a pre-construction apartment next door. The property development company allowed us to secure the apartment with a small deposit payment and additional monthly payments until the construction would be completed. Our monthly Airbnb earnings increased so fast that it would reach a point where it would outgrow my LinkedIn wage. Was this a sign?

After one year and three months at LinkedIn, I started getting restless; it was time to move on. I couldn't complain about LinkedIn as they treated me very well. I earned unlimited commissions; I joined a LinkedIn sales kick-off in Las Vegas, an introduction training in Chicago, and enjoyed numerous fun activities with colleagues. For business trips, I stayed in the nicest hotels and rented luxury cars. Everything was possible. But still, I wasn't completely satisfied. The job was stressful, days were long, and in the end, I was just filling the pockets of the shareholders. It felt a bit like being locked in a golden cage. I always dreamed of running my own business, and I knew that this was my opportunity to follow my dreams. After one year and three months, we decided to choose happiness over money and become digital nomads. I quit my job, we sold the last pieces of furniture that we owned in Ireland, and we tried to fit our lives in a couple of bags and suitcases.

We took this picture on the day we left Ireland while waiting for our taxi to the airport. It felt good but strange. A new chapter of our lives would start.

We wanted to travel the world, so we booked a one-way ticket to Hongkong. And, one of the best things was that we were making money on the go while traveling, thanks to our Airbnb Business. Our Airbnb listings generated by that time sufficient to cover our travel costs while working an average of just 2-hours daily, managing 16 listings.

After Hongkong, we traveled to Malaysia and Singapore. Then we decided to fly to Australia, where we rented a campervan and drove from Melbourne to Cairns in a couple of weeks. After Australia, we continued our trip with a visit to Bali. Bali is so incredibly cheap;

here, we could stay in a 5-star hotel compared to what a motel would cost us in Australia. After Bali, we decided to go to Thailand. We visited the full moon party, did some island hopping, and explored Bangkok. After a couple of months in Asia, we decided that we had seen enough and continued our trip to Europe. We visited the Netherlands, Belgium, Germany, England, Spain, and moved on to the USA, where we traveled along the east coast. We decided to continue our trip to the Dominican Republic to visit family and friends.

When we arrived in the Dominican Republic, we visited our apartment and, we found out that there was a beautiful one-bedroom apartment for sale in the same building. We knew that the demand was high in the area and that guests loved the building's location and facilities. Therefore, this was an excellent opportunity to expand our portfolio. We decided to go for it and visited several local banks to apply for a mortgage. Unfortunately, it didn't look that good. In the Dominican Republic, banks charge an average of 11% interest on mortgages. Buying a $100,000 property with a 30-year mortgage with 11% interest would cost us over $242,000. Our monthly payments would be around $952 for thirty years! A risky mortgage such as this would put severe pressure on the business, and the property would always have to perform well. As this wouldn't be a smart way to grow our real estate portfolio, we started looking at alternative ways to finance the property. Luckily, we found family members interested in helping us with a loan for an interest rate way lower than what the banks quoted. Property number 2 was ours and ready to be offered on Airbnb immediately.

We managed to increase our portfolio with several new properties that we would rent out for the owners on a commission base, bringing the total number of listings that we managed to 35 properties.

Our digital nomad life was great; however, we had seen enough after traveling half of the world for about one year. It sounds strange, but visiting amazing beaches, national parks, or different cities becomes ordinary after a while. Even eating out for breakfast, lunch, and dinner every day becomes routine, making you want to cook something yourself. Also, the feeling of always being on the go wasn't something we wanted to do forever. We felt that it was time to settle and build up our life in a place that we truly loved.

Some of our favorite options were Sydney, New York, and Barcelona. However, Sydney is far away from our loved ones, and New York would be a bit hectic, but Barcelona had a mix of everything we were looking for. It became our preferred option.

We both knew Barcelona very well. In 2010, we both lived here and even met in this city for the first time. Therefore, moving back six years later felt like coming home. We both loved this city. In November 2016, we moved back to Barcelona, found a beautiful apartment, and finally settled down. Now we had the time to focus on our Airbnb business and grow it to the next level.

At that time, we owned two Airbnb apartments, had a third brand new apartment in construction, and managed 35 properties. Step by step, we extended our portfolio, acquired new properties, and increased our earnings. We reached Airbnb's Superhost status (Superhosts are experienced hosts who provide a shining example for other hosts and extraordinary experiences for their guests.) soon after the program rolled out, and until today (fingers crossed), we still have the Airbnb Superhost status. At this time, we own several Airbnb properties, manage 100+ Airbnb listings, and have hosted thousands of guests. Some of our Airbnb listings are part of the exclusive Airbnb Plus homes (a program that allows Airbnb hosts to apply to receive a "Plus" classification that recognizes listings with exceptional quality, comfort, and style). We have 1400+ reviews with an average review score of 4.8 out of 5 stars, and our collection consists of luxury apartments and villas all around the Dominican Republic.

As I frequently received questions from other hosts asking for tips and advice on how to increase earnings with Airbnb, I started a short-term rental marketing and consulting company called www.RentalsMarketing.com. With Rentals Marketing, I have helped increase the revenue of hundreds of property management companies, independent hotels, and short-term rental owners from Sri Lanka to Hawaii and anywhere in between. Talking daily with short-term rental entrepreneurs, I realized that it was time to write a book and leverage my short-term rental knowledge to help other hosts.

The objective of this book is to create economic opportunity for every Airbnb host. I hope you'll enjoy this book. Happy hosting!

Brighton Beach Melbourne June 2018

Introduction

Who is this book for?

Do you want to increase your Airbnb earnings substantially? Or start a successful Airbnb business from scratch? Are you willing to put a fair share of time and effort into your Airbnb business? If the answer to the above questions is yes, then this book is for you!

Let's be clear. This book is by no means a get-rich-quick-scheme. Becoming successful on Airbnb takes considerable effort. It means wearing different hats, dealing with sales and marketing, and understanding taxes and regulations. It involves having to interact with guests and perhaps employees daily. And so much more. But if you build your Airbnb business the smart way, you could become wealthy, create passive income, or perhaps even become a digital nomad. Dare to dream!

I wrote this book for new hosts, experienced hosts, property management companies, rental arbitrage businesses, and real estate investors. But only for those that genuinely want to increase their Airbnb earnings and are willing to put in the effort needed to become a top performer in their region. Being average on Airbnb isn't enough to be successful. Therefore, in this book, I'll show you how to outperform your competition and substantially increase your Airbnb earnings.

This book is full of tips and tricks that will help you increase your Airbnb earnings when applied the right way. Most of the information in this book comes from my personal Airbnb hosting and consulting experience, running a successful Airbnb business as an Airbnb Superhost with 100+ listings, investing in real estate, and helping hundreds of Airbnb hosts increase their earnings with my marketing company www.RentalsMarketing.com. Additionally, I have read 12 books about Airbnb, so I can assure you that this book covers the essential subjects about increasing your Airbnb earnings. I look forward to helping you!

Skills of successful Airbnb hosts

Being an Airbnb host isn't for everyone. In many cases, Airbnb hosts have to be available 365 days per year, be friendly and understanding, know their numbers and enjoy what they are doing. The most successful Airbnb hosts have some of the following skills in common:

- **Communicative:** They are excellent at conveying information to others clearly and concisely (both written and verbal) while connecting with their audience.
- **Proactive.** Great Airbnb hosts get stuff done by offering immediate solutions for problems, ensuring that their properties and spaces are in top conditions, and prevent issues from happening.

- **Dynamic:** Successful hosts can easily switch between tasks and conversations. They are creative and flexible.
- **Entrepreneurial:** Successful hosts are often innovative. They come up with new ideas, concepts, businesses/or procedures to increase earnings.
- **Negotiation:** The best Airbnb hosts know how to negotiate. Especially with guests, but also with stakeholders. They ensure that guests are satisfied while keeping their Airbnb business's objectives and values in mind.
- **Finance:** Successful hosts know their numbers. They control their costs, know how to optimize for revenue, and do their taxes the correct way.
- **Marketing:** Successful Airbnb hosts understand the game of selling their property on Airbnb and marketing it to their specific target audience.

Please don't worry if you feel that you might need some work on some of the above skills. The most important thing is that you have the motivation to make hosting a success on Airbnb, and are willing to invest the time needed. Then you can work on the things listed above, even if it means that you'll need to hire someone to help you host on Airbnb. There are plenty of solutions discussed in this book.

How to use this book?

This book is a do-it-yourself guide that covers the most important aspects of hosting on Airbnb. This book will guide you step by step through Airbnb's world and teach you everything you need to know to become a successful host. I have divided this book into four main sections:

- **Find:** Understand what type of Airbnb business is most profitable for you.
- **List:** Create an engaging and optimized Airbnb listing that stands out.
- **Maximize:** Obtain top-ranking and outperform your competition while maximizing your Airbnb earnings.
- **Scale:** Grow your Airbnb business the smart way by building a successful business model that easily scales, thereby having the growth and extra income you want without the extra work.

The content in this book might be a bit overwhelming when reading at first. Therefore, I'd recommend using this book as your map to navigate through all Airbnb sections while optimizing. To obtain the best results, use this book as a handbook while working on your Airbnb profile.

What is Airbnb?

Airbnb was founded in 2007 by designers Brian Chesky and Joe Gebbia, who just moved from New York to San Francisco and couldn't afford the monthly rent on their San Francisco apartment. They noticed that almost all hotel rooms in the city were booked, as the local Industrial Design conference attracted many visitors. So they decided to turn their loft into a lodging space, rented out three air mattresses on the floor, and served breakfast. They didn't want to post on Craigslist because it felt too impersonal. Their entrepreneur instinct said, "build your own site." And so they did. They decided to make a simple website, basically a blog with maps. www.airbedandbreakfast.com was born.

AirBed&Breakfast

Book rooms with locals, rather than hotels.

The Airbnb original company logo.

Two men and one woman showed up, paying $80 each—all sleeping on an air mattress on their floor. Once the first guests left, they knew they had an incredible concept in hand.

They invited former roommate Nathan Blecharcyk, who worked as a Technical Architect, to become a co-founder and build the site. They re-launched the website for the yearly SXSW - South by Southwest festival in Austin, but disappointingly only got two bookings.

In the context of the Airbnb startup story, generating revenue and finding investors came from an unusual source. Since the "bed" part of "bed and breakfast" wasn't successful yet, Chesky thought of focusing on the business's breakfast side. Taking advantage of the election fever, Chesky and Gebbia came up with the idea of creating presidential-themed breakfast cereals – The Obama O's; The Breakfast of Change, and Captain McCain's; A Maverick in Every Bite. The founders handcrafted and sold each limited-edition cereal box for $40 apiece. The cereal box idea goes down in the Airbnb startup story as the break that kept the company afloat for a few more months. The cereal boxes' earnings almost pulled the company out of debt and gained Airbnb some national press coverage.

In November 2008, Paul Graham, founder of Y Combinator (provides seed funding for startups), wasn't convinced that the Airbnb business model would work. But through the presidential-themed cereal boxes, the venture capitalist was impressed by the founders' creativity and passion. In 2009 they got $20,000 funding from Paul Graham's Y Combinator.

They were making around $200 weekly for months, not growing much. Finally, they realized a potential reason for the lack of growth: the listings' photos were not that appealing. So, they went door-to-door in New York City and took pictures of listed houses. One week later, turnover had doubled to $400 weekly. They saw growth finally. However, they were rejected by a famous Venture Capitalist, Fred Wilson, in New York, but then Barry Manilow's drummer rented out an entire house. This made them realize that Airbnb would be more than just renting out air mattresses. The company then started growing fast after receiving a $600,000 investment from Sequoia Capital. In 2010, they raised $7.2 million, and in 2011, another $112 million from many investors, including Ashton Kutcher.

Airbnb was not the first online "couch-surfing and unique accommodations" site. Far from it. Airbnb's founders weren't seasoned tech pros; two of the three were art students at the Rhode Island School of Design. So how did the company take off so fast? Because Airbnb solved a critical problem, the lack of well-priced housing. And they executed it the right way; they focused on building a simple to use platform, excellent customer service, and appealing listings by adding quirkier spaces such as houseboats, treehouses, and castles. They also showed host information, thereby making it more personal. Millennials were drawn to the new way of travel that was both adventurous and affordable. You could stay in someone's home within the conventional tourism grid while connecting with like-minded people at the cost of much less than an average hotel stay. On top of that, Airbnb offered people an opportunity to monetize their homes by becoming so-called "hosts" on the platform. All these factors helped Airbnb to grow at a swift pace.

But success didn't come easy. Over the years, Airbnb has also dealt with all the unintended consequences of putting strangers together, including attacks, theft, and lack of responsibility on the part of its hosts. Additionally, in recent years, the company has had to confront racism and other discrimination types on the platform. Airbnb is also still dealing with perhaps their biggest obstacle: in many cities and municipalities worldwide, the fundamental activity enabled by Airbnb - individuals renting out a room or a complete home for a short time, is illegal. In recent years, local laws in many of the largest cities and municipalities have made it much more complicated for Airbnb hosts to rent out spaces. Claiming that Airbnb is having a detrimental impact on housing stock as it encourages landlords to move their properties out from the long-term rental and for-sale markets into the short-term rental market, resulting in increased home prices and rents in some of the world's highest-demanded areas.

At the same time, Airbnb's usage has exploded well beyond the millennial demographic. These days, Airbnb is not just used by celebrities such as Beyoncé and Britney Spears, forgoing five-star hotels for opulent Airbnb estates, but also baby boomers, seniors, and so many other people worldwide. Airbnb has redefined how we travel, opening a new market for alternative accommodations. And now, Airbnb is aiming to change how we experience new places and how we live our lives at home. It has done so many things against the odds, and all because of the three guys that had this creative idea to resolve their problem - paying the rent!

According to Airbnb, in 2021, the company has:

- 7+ Million listings to stay
- Available in 220 countries and 100,000+ cities Worldwide
- Hosts sharing their homes have earned over $80 billion
- Airbnb has had over half a billion guest arrivals all-time
- Airbnb offers over 40,000 Experiences around the world
- An average of 2 million guests are staying daily in an Airbnb

A Morgan Stanley study has shown that the top reasons for people to use Airbnb are:

- To save costs on accommodation
- Because of the location
- Because of the authentic experience
- Because of the easy to use site/app

Airbnb brings enormous opportunities for hosts to earn a nice side income or build a professional business. As Airbnb is growing up, so are its hosts. The average listing quality is improving; prices are becoming more competitive, the offering increases rapidly, and hosts are starting to use software to increase earnings and automate processes.

This also brings challenges to the table, such as local regulations, intense competition, and lower average nightly rates, leaving hosts with two options. To either go for it the full 100%, become a top Airbnb host, or slowly see competitors taking over. When Jennifer and I started renting our apartments out on Airbnb, almost anything would sell. We could have lousy photos, half furnished listings, or weak descriptions, and still, we would get tons of bookings for average nightly rates higher than they are now. Competition has increased, and so has professionalism increased, with most of the best Airbnb listings being hosted by professional hosts or companies with multiple listings. They often use professional photography, professionally designed properties, automation, technology such as pricing tools, etc. They are making it more challenging to compete. Being successful on Airbnb is an ongoing process. We are slowly moving towards a market where the winners take it all. The winners will be the most active hosts with the best quality properties, completed profiles, competitive pricing, the highest review scores, and the best processes in place.

1. Find: How to choose your rental property?

" Understand what type of Airbnb business is most profitable for you. "

This chapter is mainly written for hosts that still must decide upon how to start from scratch. If you already have a location, property, or established business, I'd recommend to scan through this chapter and only read the relevant information.

Your Airbnb business model

Before publishing your Airbnb listing, choose carefully how and what you'd like to rent out. In this chapter, I'll discuss what to consider when selecting your favorite Airbnb business model, the type of property, location, quality, design, and other essential details you should think about before becoming an Airbnb host.

Are you an aspiring Airbnb host? Or are you already hosting on Airbnb and looking for new ways to increase your income by expanding your property portfolio? Choose your rental property wisely. These are the most common Airbnb business models:

Property owner model

When you list a property that you own entirely or partly on Airbnb, some of the advantages are:

- **Maximize earnings:** When listing a property you own on Airbnb, the earnings will be yours, allowing you to maximize your Airbnb earnings versus your invested time.
- **Appreciation:** How much a property appreciates each year depends on the local real estate market and its improvements. Traditionally, investing in real estate is considered a long-term safe investment, as property values tend to rise over time.

Some of the disadvantages are:

- **Recessions and other disasters**: Such as the COVID-19 pandemic, can put you in financial trouble when there is suddenly a decrease in demand for your listing. If you don't have a mortgage to pay or have high fixed costs, it wouldn't necessarily be a big problem. However, if you do, you must find an alternative way to pay for your mortgage and cover your costs. Also, bear in mind that the value of your property might decrease during these times.
- **Regulations:** Short-term rental laws often change; this could be a potential threat for your business, especially when financing your property with a mortgage or loan. Therefore,

you should always have a back-up plan. What would you do with your property if Airbnb would be banned starting tomorrow?

- **Maintenance:** When purchasing a property that isn't in perfect conditions, you'll likely have to invest in maintenance or remodeling sooner or later. Keep in mind that while your property is being remodeled, you won't be able to rent it out, which will result in a decrease in earnings.

Rental arbitrage model

The act of leasing a property long-term and then re-renting it on a short-term basis. Some of the advantages are:

- **Return on investment:** If you don't own any real estate, but have little savings and are looking for a high return on investment Airbnb business model, then this might be your way of hosting on Airbnb. Try to rent a property for the lowest possible monthly price, and try to sell it nightly for the highest reasonable price; the difference between the rent price and the selling price is yours.

- **Scalability:** Once you have a successful Airbnb rental arbitrage business, it is relatively easy to scale. Find new homes, list them on Airbnb, and optimize their performance and earnings.

Some of the most important disadvantages are:

- **Win fast, lose fast:** The downside of Airbnb rental arbitrage is that you can lose money just as quickly as you can make money. As with all other arbitrage forms, sometimes buying low and selling high does not go according to plan. In this case, you'll often have to sign a lease for a year, if not years. If the business doesn't go as planned, local regulations change, etc., you'll still be responsible for paying the property's monthly rent.
- **Startup costs:** Security deposits, furniture, legal, and application fees are some of the expenses that come with preparing a rental arbitrage property as a short-term rental.
- **Difficult to find:** Finding a landlord that is okay with you renting out their property on Airbnb is one of the biggest challenges for Airbnb rental arbitrage hosts. Most landlords don't see the benefits for themselves. Therefore, you might have to convince them with higher monthly payments.

Property management model

The act of listing someone else's property on Airbnb and then charging them a fixed fee or commission percentage of the earnings. Some of the most important advantages are:

- **Startup costs:** You can start a property management business model with very little to no startup costs. Simply find property owners with furnished properties, and convince them to let you rent out their property for a commission or a fixed fee per reservation.

- **No cure, no pay:** No risk for you. If you don't bring in any bookings, you won't have to pay for anything.
- **Scalability:** This is a very scalable business model if created the right way. You can easily manage multiple properties alone. Just advertise the listings the right way, and ensure that you are on top of business. If you decide to offer additional property management services such as cleaning, maintenance, or key-handovers, things may get more complicated and time-consuming.

Some of the most important disadvantages are:

- **Losing properties:** If you don't bring in enough business, the property owner will likely stop working with you or find someone else to list/rent their property.
- **Restrictions:** If a property owner sets you certain limitations such as rates that aren't competitive or complicated minimum length of stay restrictions, then this might prevent the property from getting booked.
- **Guest satisfaction:** When offering a property on a commission base, likely, you aren't in control of the property quality (furniture, maintenance, etc.). If the property you list on Airbnb isn't in good conditions, then this might cause bad reviews and guest complaints, affecting your Airbnb account

and, in the worst case, the performance of your other Airbnb listings.

Airbnb co-hosting

Co-hosting on Airbnb falls under the property management model. Airbnb co-hosts help other Airbnb hosts take care of their property and guests in exchange for a fixed fee or commission percentage of their earnings. Airbnb hosts can give someone else permission to access specific Airbnb listing functionalities, such as assigning tasks, guest management, listing management, finances, and team management. Co-hosts are often experienced hosts helping non-experienced hosts or hosts who don't have the time to manage their listings.

Choose your Airbnb business model carefully

Each one of these Airbnb business models has definite advantages and disadvantages. Investigate your options carefully and choose which business model suits you best.

For our Airbnb business, we decided to mix our rental portfolio and offer all three options. The properties we own are the moneymakers; they produce around 40% of our yearly net income. We decided to do rental arbitrage for one property. It was a huge opportunity due to the low monthly rent we are paying to the owner and the high monthly earnings the property generates. But we have invested $10,000 decorating the property, and that is always a risk. We decided to apply the property management model to most properties due to the low risk. To maintain our high reputation on Airbnb, we chose only to offer luxury listings and outstanding price/quality options that provide high standards. This way, we would ensure high quality and prevent bad reviews affecting our Superhost status and other listings' performance.

Some property owners have asked us to offer extra services such as cleaning, maintenance, key handovers, etc. Coordinating and organizing these services is very time consuming and won't produce that much revenue, so we decided not to offer them. To run an Airbnb business that is as effective and efficient as possible, we applied the 80/20 rule. 20% of the work generates 80% of the income. It is the marketing that's the sweet spot for us. Therefore, we choose to only offer marketing and guest communication services to the property owners. The property owners oversee the cleaning and maintenance themselves. It allows us to run this business remotely.

When hosting on Airbnb, think very carefully about how you'd like to build your business. You could invest in real estate if your market is right. This way, you can maximize your Airbnb earnings and invest in an asset that possibly increases in value long term. This way, instead of paying rent, you are generating money for your business just by paying your mortgage.

The perfect location

Once you have decided which Airbnb business model(s) you'd like to use, it is time to look at your property's ideal location. I'd recommend taking the following factors in mind when choosing the perfect place:

- **Legal regulations:** Is it allowed to offer short-term rentals in your preferred area? Are there any national or local laws that will affect your short-term rental business? Investigate if anything may indicate future regulations or laws that could complicate your short-term rental business. For instance, we live in Barcelona, and here, it is only allowed to offer a property as a short-term rental when it has a touristic license number. Currently, the government doesn't provide these licenses anymore. The only option to obtain a license is to purchase a property that already has one.

- **Demand:** Your property could be the best Airbnb in the world, but if it is somewhere no one is looking to stay, you will be out of business soon. I'd recommend starting your Airbnb business in a popular area with high demand, as this will bring you more opportunities to increase occupancy.

- **Competition:** How much competition is there in your area? Also, on a property level. Are most properties one-bedroom apartments or multi-room family homes?

- **Guests:** What type of guests are traveling to your preferred area? Are these business travelers or tourists?
- **Seasonality:** How do you think the short-term rental conditions are year-round? If your property is in a winter sports area, you'll likely see less demand in the summer.
- **Pricing:** How is your competition priced? Do your math carefully and calculate how much your property could sell for in that market.
- **Expenses:** Calculate your costs. How much will you have to spend on taxes, insurance, cleaning, water, electricity, wifi, etc.?

How to get the answers to these points mentioned above? Here are some helpful tips and ideas:

- **Use Airbnb:** Search for the listings in your area - how many listings are there? How many reviews do they have? How are they priced? Open their calendars and check how many days are available for the next couple of days.
- **Tax advisor:** Talk to a local tax advisor about the Airbnb taxes in your area.
- **Tourism board:** See if the local tourism board has information about the type of travelers, length of stay, high and low seasons, etc.
- **Google maps:** Are there events, touristic highlights, or large businesses in the area that might attract Airbnb guests?

- **Data:** Use a data company like www.AirDNA.co to find Airbnb statistics about your local market. They even have a free version which already offers some great insights, such as the number of Airbnb listings in the area you are looking for.
- **Google:** Search for articles, local newspapers, or local government websites, and try to find as much as you can about Airbnb or short-term rentals in your area.

The company AirDNA researched the USA's best cities for Airbnb hosts; these are their findings: www.airdna.co/blog/best-cities-for-airbnb. Not every city can be an Airbnb hit. I live in Barcelona, but our properties are in the Caribbean. I would love to build our Airbnb business in Barcelona. Unfortunately, Barcelona's local regulations that often change make it relatively complicated and risky to create a short-term rental company from scratch. This is why we decided to grow our business in the Caribbean instead of expanding to other continents.

I often hear from people that they prefer not to invest in areas with many existing Airbnb listings. In their opinion, it is more difficult to get booked in these areas. They might be wrong! Due to the high demand and good return on investment, some areas have much more Airbnb listings than others. You can be very successful in these markets, even as a new host. Just ensure that you do a better job than your competition. Airbnb's ranking is just like Google's ranking; the best performing listings get the highest-ranking and often the most clicks.

Your target market

Once you have found the perfect area for your Airbnb listing, think about what type of guests will travel here and what kind of property they might be looking for. Hosts often don't look at the location from the guest's perspective, resulting in guests being disappointed by areas for not meeting expectations. Usually, this happens due to subjective preferences like neighborhood, community, convenience, peacefulness, accuracy, security, ambiance, connectivity, or access. Therefore, think carefully about your target guests. Are they interested in staying at your exact location? Also, ensure to set expectations the right way in your Airbnb listing.

Your property type

Have you decided what Airbnb business model you'd like to use and already found the perfect location for it? Did you already think of the property type you'd like to offer? Airbnb categorizes properties into the following four property types:

- **Entire place:** Guests have the whole place to themselves. This usually includes a bedroom, a bathroom, and a kitchen. Hosts should note in the description if they are on the property.
- **Private room**: Guests have a private room for sleeping. Other areas could be shared.

- **Hotel room:** A private or shared room for instance, in a boutique hotel or hostel.
- **Shared room**: Guests sleep in a bedroom or a common area that could be shared with others.

Not only does Airbnb allow you to rent out traditional properties such as apartments or homes, but it is also possible to rent almost any type of space where guests can sleep, such as cabins, chalets, castles, igloos, and treehouses.

According to Airbnb, the most popular property in the world listed on the platform is not a loft in Manhattan or a beachfront apartment in Rio de Janeiro. It's a tiny "mushroom dome" in Aptos, California.

The Mushroom Dome Retreat in California: www.airbnb.es/rooms/8357.

Be creative! Having a unique Airbnb can be a very profitable business. How do you pick your holiday spots? Weather? Value for money? You most likely have various factors at play. A study in the UK has shown that the number one reason millennials consider when choosing a holiday destination is how Instagrammable it is. This might also explain why unique places - such as the California Dome Retreat - are incredibly popular on Airbnb and often are fully booked months in advance for steep nightly rates.

Property quality

No matter what type of property or space you are listing on Airbnb, you must ensure that the basics are right; is there a place to sleep? Is it clean and safe? If your listing's basic quality is average or below average, you'll have a difficult time generating money on Airbnb. You might get bad reviews that will affect your ranking, conversion (how many guests look at your listing versus how many book your listing). And as a result, you might have to lower your rates to motivate guests to book. It is not a good idea to go down this path, therefore ensure that the basics are right. Essential amenities are the most important fundamental items that a guest expects to have a comfortable stay. These include:

- Toilet paper
- Soap (for hands and body)
- One towel per guest
- One pillow per guest
- Linens for each guest bed

Offering essential amenities is a small investment that will help increase guest satisfaction.

Interior design

Hosts often look at Airbnb interior design as an expense and not an investment. Keep in mind that part of the appeal of booking on Airbnb is the variety of homes someone can choose from, with looks and styles that are highly individualized. Airbnb interviewed many guests about their opinions towards interior design and discovered a common theme: guests consistently choose Airbnb because there's something unique about the spaces that make them feel at home. But what does that mean? How do we quantify this feeling?

Airbnb defines a home as a space that feels cared for and loved. A space with a person behind it who recognizes and welcomes guests. An Airbnb home should be a safe haven when exploring new places. It should feel comfortable, with a soul and story to tell.

It's a common misconception that Airbnb homes should only have standard looking designs and furniture pieces to appeal to a broader audience, like styling for an open house for a real estate sale. Research by Airbnb has shown that guests preferred the opposite. Creating a blank slate makes sense if you're trying to sell a house because visitors can visualize their own lives in the space. But if a guest is looking to live like a local for a short visit, being in a home that feels lived in has a significant positive impact on their experience.

For homes that follow a generic model, it can be hard to stand out from the crowd because the only differentiation at that point is the price, and trust me, that's not the battle you want to fight. Airbnb's most popular listings have something in common: they're incredibly unique and tell stories about the host or location: https://news.airbnb.com/the-most-wish-listed-homes-of-the-past-decade/.

These homes become a destination in and of themselves, and people go out of their way to plan trips around the ability to stay in them. Airbnb also found that hosts who highlight their passions within the space are more likely to connect with guests who share similar interests.

Ultimately, it's the look and feel of an Airbnb listing that sets it apart from the competition. The look and feel may be representing the host and their passions while also telling the story of the location or a theme. Airbnb likes your property interior design to:

- Avoid sterile or empty spaces
- Create collections that highlight your passion
- Consider a statement piece
- Showcase your personality
- Show plants and flowers adding vibrancy
- Create a cohesive look by using colors, textiles, artwork, and welcoming details

As the points above still leave plenty of space for questions and interpretations, I created a list with more specific recommendations that will help you identify what design works best for your listing:

Who will visit your area?

You'll need to identify your target audience so that you can tailor your decor to their desire and needs. The first step is figuring out who exactly will be visiting your area. Would guests travel to your location for business or leisure? Find out who your audience is by looking at the highest-ranked Airbnb's within your area and checking what they focus on in their descriptions, photos, and recommendations. Check with the local tourist information center if there are any statistics available about arrivals in nearby airports. Also, check if your listings are close to polar tourism highlights, convention centers, or perhaps the financial district. These could be all indicators of certain types of guests wanting to stay in your area.

Who would you like to host?

Once you have figured out what type of travelers visit your area, you should figure out what kind of travelers would be your primary target group. If you have a 5-bedroom home, you are more likely to have families or groups visiting your home, then business travels. Also, take in mind if you'd like to focus on the low, mid, or high-end market with your listing. Finding your ideal target group doesn't mean that you should not accept bookings from other travelers. It will just help you to take advantage of meeting the demand by offering the right product.

Why would they like to stay at your home?

Once you have defined your target audience, ask yourself why guests would want to stay in your home? Is it because of the fantastic location, stunning views, a rooftop pool, or a spacious garden?

Once you have cleared this out, you should know who would stay in your area, why they visit your location, and why they want to stay at your property. Now it is time to design your property in a way that these guests will feel at home.

How to design the interior and exterior of your property?

When designing your property, think like your guests, not like yourself. It might be tempting to choose items that you like, but try to keep your tastes out of the decision-making process. The only thing that matters is that your guests think it looks nice. Some great interior and exterior design tips are:

Step 1. Choose a theme for your listing.

Choose a theme that compliments your Airbnb's surroundings. This could be as simple as choosing the primary colors for your property, the type of interior design - modern, classic, warm, or cold. This could also go as far as choosing to design your home with a unique gimmick or pattern, such as a pirate, star wars, lego, or perhaps a gamers theme. When selecting your theme, endeavor to be consistent from room to room, and choose decorative and practical items of the same colors on a note to ensure to include the much-needed items for

44

your target guest without diverting from your theme—looking for inspiration? Go to www.pinterest.com and search for interior design. You'll find thousands of unique interior designs that will give you inspiration for your home.

Step 2. Design your space for comfort.
A good design is essential for your success on Airbnb, but even more important, you want your guests to feel as though your space has been thoughtfully designed, with their needs in mind. Use furniture and details that are comfortable and, at the same time, look appealing.

Step 3. Don't be afraid to get creative.
The goal is to make your Airbnb listing stand out, and there are plenty of adventurous guests looking for a space with a wow factor. You might choose to brighten rooms with eye-catching colors, creating visual impact by suspensive interesting items from ceiling beams to the use of over-the-top artwork.

Step 4. Add warmth with personal touches.
Do you have a beach home? Neutral pale blues and tans would provide that peaceful feeling that is reminiscent of the beach. Some shells, a beach umbrella, and colorful flowers will give the space that additional warm touch. Do you have a city home? Help your guests relax by going with a friendly, clean, and modern theme. Cities are often bold, challenging, and bright, so your Airbnb should be without going overboard. Add some color, and look for details like vases, photo frames, wall art, books, and creative lighting.

Step 5. Dress up the windows.

Stay away from roller blinds. Heavier curtains work well and add warmth to a room, which is especially important for the winter months. For the bedroom, make sure you use blackout curtains. Your guests would highly appreciate it.

Step 6. Style with flowers and greenery.

Adding flowers and plants to your property will improve the entire vibe of your space. Plants are alive; they stand tall and bright and can fill your property with purified air and positivity. There are plenty of relatively indestructible plants, meaning they can take a long-time without water, sunlight, or additional nutrition. Some options are Aloe Vera, Parlor Palm, Yucca, or the Neon Pothos. Only use real plants and flowers if they will be well kept. Even these plants will need some water occasionally. If you are not sure of keeping them alive, you are better off with artificial ones.

Step 7. Embrace smaller spaces.

Instead of pulling out all the stops to make a space look more spacious, try embracing the smallness! Create a cozy reading corner that guests wouldn't want to abandon or a comfortable music library hangout filled with cushions.

Step 8. Make it instagrammable.

As mentioned before, a recent study has revealed that 40% of millennials choose a travel spot based on its instagrammability. Be it the colorful coast of Positano or Maldives' turquoise seas, it's all about getting those precious likes, leading to more followers. Location plays an important role here. However, by incorporating a unique design into your home that gives it that Instagrammable touch, you can take full advantage of the demand. Think about specific places where you can achieve these fun ideas, including a unique bath in your listing, a cozy lounge corner, a cinema room, or unique artwork on the walls.

Step 9. Avoid white walls.

Be brave and choose a unique wallpaper or warm paint colors on feature walls. Pinterest can help you with lots of outside-the-box ideas. Try painting half and half walls; for example, selecting a bold color like Bordeaux red and pairing it with a toned-down shade like Egyptian Grey.

Step 10. Mix up textures and budgets.

Use a mix of more expensive statement furniture pieces mixed with unique secondhand items to create curiosity and interest. Diverse interior styles are a huge trend and can be fun if they are well selected! Explore local second-hand shops, vintage stores, or your grandparents' lofts to find the best items. If the color isn't right? Paint it.

Step 11. Invest in unique lighting.

Hanging lighting completes a tailor-made look and is often the central element in a room. Glass pendants are also an excellent option for something a bit more special. Ensure that there are plenty of warm-colored lamps for mood lighting throughout the home, and always include bedside lamps or wall lights in the bedrooms for nighttime reading. When choosing the light bulbs, go for warm white and soft light that gives your space that warm and cozy feeling.

Step 12. White bedsheets.

Always use white bedsheets. It is a psychological thing and no coincidence that hotels, in general, use white linen. White bed sheets communicate cleanliness; you can add colored pillows or blankets for some colors.

Step 13. Decorative pillows.

Decorative pillows are a great way to bring your space alive. To create a versatile base, start with a pair of neutral-tone pillows, either 20- or 22-inch squares, which feel comfortably plush. On more spacious sofas, use 18-inch squared cushions to create a versatile foundation. For the base pillows, choose a texture that interestingly plays against your sofa. Smooth linen squares look great against a sofa's crisp cotton slipcover.

Step 14. Outdoor spaces.

Take full advantage of outdoor spaces; you would want your outdoor space to be inviting and contain durable items to withstand the weather. Having an outdoor seating area is an excellent add-on for any Airbnb listing. Add a dining table, umbrella, barbecue, chimney, firepit, or lounge chairs so that guests can use the outdoor space. Important: take in mind your neighbors - not all outdoor spaces are suited for barbecue, chimneys, or firepits.

Step 15. Mirrors.

Mirrors will make all spaces look more spacious. They can also be used as unique style elements, for instance, when choosing fashionable round mirrors or using oversized leaning mirrors. Make sure they are functional, too, by installing them at the right height.

What to avoid:

- **Overkill:** Some overkill examples are; a pelican in every picture, a seashell on every wall, or only red walls. Moderation is key.
- **Clutter:** Simplicity is best, plus fewer items mean less cleaning and fewer things that could potentially break.
- **Personal items:** Put away your private family photos and odds that guests wouldn't use or understand.
- **Religious items:** You are likely to have guests from various beliefs and values; therefore, it is better to remove religious items that could make them feel uncomfortable or unwelcome.
- **Expensive or sentimental items:** Take in mind that things might break. It is recommendable not to place items that are expensive or irreplaceable in your home.

Professionally design your home

If interior design isn't your strength, reach out to a company in your area that can help you design your home. Searching on google for local interior design companies, you'll likely find some options. Ensure that you work with a fixed rate per project to know how much you'll be spending on fees. If you don't want any surprises, ask for their portfolio, and be clear about your budget. Most companies will charge for their services, starting at a couple of hundreds up to a couple of thousand dollars. Don't forget, investing in professional interior design is an investment that will likely bring you more income through Airbnb. Some great remote interior design companies are:

- **Havenly:** www.havenly.com
- **Decorist:** www.decorist.com
- **Modsy:** www.modsy.com

Are you planning to decorate your property yourself? Some of the following tips might help you out:

- **Unique pieces**: Furniture outlets or second-hand stores are great places to pick up different elements.
- **Ikea:** An excellent place for decoration shopping. Just keep in mind that you won't be the only Airbnb host having Ikea decoration.
- **Airbnb furniture packages:** Yes, it is even possible to buy complete Airbnb furniture packages for all your rooms. If you don't have the budget to hire an interior designer and don't know much about putting the right furniture together, then this might be an option for you. Just remember that you won't be the only person buying that furniture package.
- **Leasing furniture:** Do you have little or no money to invest? Leasing furniture might be an option for you. With relatively low risk and little cash on the table, you can start renting your space with decent furniture paid with a payment plan.

Expert tip: When decorating your property, take advantage of stores that offer 0% financing. This way, you can decorate your property without having to spend the money upfront. Instead, you'll pay later or monthly. Also, take advantage of seasonal specials or sales. Is Black Friday coming soon? Take advantage and purchase with steep discounts.

We have professionally designed properties in our portfolio with unique decoration, artwork, colors, textiles, and welcoming details. And we have non-professional designed properties with a more basic trim, fewer colors, no artwork, and only a few details. The professionally interior designed properties are performing better on Airbnb. They get more reservations at higher average rates than the non-professional listings, giving all else is equal. Additionally, they tend to get higher review scores than the more generic-looking spaces. In the long run, our professionally designed listings generate a higher return on investment. Consider hiring a professional interior designer; this is an investment that should increase your earnings on Airbnb.

2. List: How to create the perfect Airbnb listing?

"Create an engaging and optimized Airbnb listing that stands out."

Creating the perfect Airbnb listing is both art and science. It has to look well and make sense. You could have done everything right, but if you mess up your Airbnb listing, your property won't get booked. Your listing is how potential guests find and book the space you want to share.

Important: To maximize the completeness of your Airbnb listing and profile, in this chapter, I cover all Airbnb profile tabs, sections, and details, including specific instructions on where to go to make the suggested updates and changes. Airbnb frequently changes the platform; therefore, some of these sections, tabs, or details might not exist anymore, might have different names, or might have been moved around. If you can't find the suggested information, then I'd recommend you verify on www.airbnb.com/help/home if this information is still relevant or exists.

Listing details

In this section, I will uncover the essential components you need to create the perfect Airbnb listing. You'll find tons of tips and tricks that you can instantly apply to your Airbnb account. Therefore, I'd recommend using this chapter as a guide while correcting and updating your Airbnb profile immediately while reading.

Ranking & conversion

A well created Airbnb profile will help increase your listings' ranking and booking conversion rate. Having a high ranking on Airbnb is essential for getting booked as most guests will only look at the first couple of properties that show up in their search. Additionally, a great Airbnb listing will convert "lookers into bookers!" Meaning: if your listing visitors like your listing profile, they are more likely to book it. Your mission is to have as many visitors as possible visiting your listing and booking it. When creating your profile, take in mind that every checkbox, setting, or description tab is an opportunity to sell. ABC - always be closing!

Photos

To find the "Photos" tab in Airbnb. Log in to your Airbnb account on a computer, select "Manage listing(s)," open your listing, click on "Listing details," and open the "Photos" tab.

In the "Photos" tab, you can upload and adjust your Airbnb listing photos. Photos play a crucial role in helping potential guests book accommodations online. Since they haven't seen your property in person, they rely heavily on the images you upload to help them decide. According to Airbnb, research has shown that:

- Hosts with professional photos tend to earn 40% more than other hosts without professional photos in their area.
- Photos are one of the top reasons guests choose to book and results in an average of 24% more bookings.
- Many hosts can raise their nightly prices after upgrading their photos. The average increase is 26%.

Example: John has a one-bedroom apartment with poor quality photos listed on Airbnb that rents for $100 a night with an average monthly occupancy of 60%. John earns around $100 × 18 nights (60% × 30 Nights) = $1800 monthly. John decides that it is time to improve his Airbnb listing and invests $500 in a professional photoshoot providing him with 30 spectacular photos of the interior of his apartment, exterior, and building facilities. According to Airbnb research, his monthly earnings might increase. Before the photoshoot, John earned about $1800 monthly. Airbnb suggests that John could earn up to 40% more. $1800 × 140% = $2520. Airbnb is suggesting that in this example, John's listing could increase earnings up to $720 monthly. John would earn back his professional photoshoot of $500 within less than a month. There are many other factors involved; however, my point is to show you the potentially huge impact of professional photography on your Airbnb listing.

According to Airbnb, studies have shown that up to 92% of Airbnb visitors are more likely to book properties that display high-quality professional photos. Photos are the single most crucial thing guests look at when deciding to stay at a property. It is true that on Airbnb, an image is worth a thousand words. Potential guests decide within 10 seconds if they like a property or not, majorly depending on the photos.

Also, take in mind that guests are trying to picture themselves at your property when looking at your photos. Therefore, your photos must be reflecting your listing the correct way.

If you'd ask me the single most important investment for your Airbnb listing, I would say professional photography. You can have everything right, but without great photos, you will miss out on many bookings. If hiring a professional photographer isn't an option for you, then I'd recommend using your smartphone.

Find a professional photographer

Hire an Airbnb photographer or find one yourself. These are your options:

Airbnb photography

Airbnb offers professional photography in many destinations worldwide. Log in to your Airbnb account and visit: www.airbnb.com/professional_photography. When scrolling down the page, you can see if your listing(s) are eligible for professional photography. Generally, Airbnb photographers charge anywhere between $80 for a single room and up to $500 for a villa taking an average of 2-3 photos per room. Keep in mind that you don't know in advance who will be doing the photoshoot. I have personally used Airbnb photography for over 20 listings with about six different photographers. We are generally happy with the results, only in some cases, the photo quality was below expectations.

Hire a professional photographer

When hiring a professional photographer, you should hire a photographer who is specialized in real estate photography. Almost everyone knows or can recommend you a great photographer. However, an event or wedding photographer often works with very different cameras and lenses or might have less knowledge about real estate photography. When hiring a photographer, ask for their portfolio to see if you like their work. Be clear about how many photos you'd like to have, what details are essential for you, and explain to your photographer about your property's unique selling points so they can take that in mind. Always confirm a fixed price in advance and the number of photos included. It is recommendable to have at least ten photos for a room, twenty or more photos for an apartment, and thirty or more photos for a home or villa.

How to prepare your property for a professional photoshoot

To make the most out of your photo session, ensure that the following key points are right:

1. **Damages:** Your property must be in good condition. Freshly painted and not have visible cracks or damages.
2. **Clean:** Your property should be immaculate. The windows should be clean, the floor shiny, and the kitchen spotless.
3. **Organize:** Organize your home, hide personal items, prepare the beds with fresh linen, position your furniture, and details.
4. **Stage:** Showcase what your Airbnb listing has to offer and ensure that your space looks inviting:
   - Living Area. Prepare the dining table as if guests are ready to sit down and have dinner. Stage your sofa for comfort with pillows and blankets, as if guests are to rest there. Does your home have great lightning? Turn it on. Does your listing have stunning views? Open the curtains—lay books on the coffee table. Set up a fruit bowl or wine bottle and glasses on the coffee table or kitchen counter. Hide wires. Turn the tv off and open the doors to your balcony or terrace.

- Kitchen. Show off attracting amenities such as a Nespresso coffee maker, perhaps free amenities such as coffee or tea? Clean the shining surfaces well.

- Bedroom. Open curtains, clean windows. Take out wrinkles from the bed. Put several pillows on each bed and an additional blanket—open doors to the balcony.

- Outdoor area. Only take photos outside if the weather is right. Preferably, it should be sunny with a blue sky. Ensure that there are no leaves or dirt and that the outdoor furniture looks organized and prepared with cushions etc.

5. **Brief your photographer:** Ensure that your photographer knows your home's target audience and unique selling points.

Expert tip: Airbnb prefers photos taken with natural daylight, opened curtains, and lights off. I always ask our photographer to take photos with the curtains open/closed and lights off/on. Particularly, bedroom photos often look stunning with the curtains closed and all lights on. It could give a warm and welcoming touch to your photos, while photos taken with the lights turned off, and curtains opened might feel colder and less inviting.

Curtains closed.   Curtains open.

Take Airbnb listing photos yourself

It is highly recommended to have a professional photographer take your Airbnb photos. If this isn't an option, and you'll be taking the photos yourself. Then keep in mind these tips:

Auto mode

Always use auto mode on your smartphone's camera, unless you consider yourself a pro and take better photos without the auto mode.

HDR mode on

Most smartphones and cameras come with an HDR (High Dynamic Range) mode. This is one of the most important settings when taking photos for your Airbnb listing. Have you ever taken a photo in a room with a bright window? Have you noticed how the bright window makes the rest of the room look dark or oversaturated? This is what HDR fixes. HDR mode takes several photos in rapid succession at different exposures and blends them. All the dark and oversaturated places in the photo will be bright with detail as well as the windows.

Non-HDR   HDR

Resolution matters

Airbnb recommends taking photos that are at least 1024×683px. When in doubt, bigger photos are better.

Landscape

Take your photos in landscape format. Images in the Airbnb search results are all displayed in landscape, so vertical photos won't showcase your space that well.

Take photos during the daytime

Humans are drawn to light and want to see the place they're looking at naturally. Be sure to open any blinds or shades and get any additional lighting sources fired up.

Highlight unique amenities

Guests love to stay in unique spaces with character, so call attention to details like artwork, a fireplace, or a treehouse.

Show accessibility features

Highlight features that are helpful to guests with limited mobility, such as wide doorways, step-free floors, and grab rails.

Shoot into a corner

Shooting a photo from the corners creates diagonal lines that draw people's eyes to the main focal point. Intersecting diagonal lines also gives a photo more depth and perspective.

Think symmetrically

Symmetry makes your unique pieces stand out. Think about all the elements together – harmony, lines, and balance.

Creating space

If you are taking photos of the complete room, step back as much as you can to have a comprehensive view of the space. Wide-angle shots often work best.

Waist level

Hold your phone or camera to your waist level and always point straight ahead in the room. Not up and not down.

Find your angle

Not every property will look beautiful from every angle. Find out how your property looks best from each place by taking several photos from each corner. If you mention that your place is spacious, roomy, or anything of that sort, then be sure to avoid angles that make your place look cramped or tiny.

Use grid settings

An excellent technique for taking Airbnb photos is the rule of thirds. This is where you use a grid tool on your camera, which provides a focal point in the right areas. It's an approach often used by professional photographers. For best results, place your focal point where two grid lines meet. This draws the eye and encourages the person viewing the photo to look around.

How many photos should you take?

Take lots of photos of all spaces your guests can use. Use the corners to take photos of the complete room, and add symmetric photos and close-ups to complete your photo session. The goal is to have around 2-5 great photos per room, including bathrooms, kitchen, hallway, balcony, living room, bedrooms, and the exterior. Also, take photos of all spaces your guests will have access to, including shared facilities, such as a pool, gym, terrace, garden, surroundings, and nearby highlights. Take at least ten photos per room/space to ensure that you can choose 2-5 of the best photos afterward.

Expert tip: The hour just after sunrise and before sunset is known as the 'golden hour.' This is when the sunlight is softer, and the colors are more vibrant. Although there is a small time frame of opportunity, it is an excellent time for shooting outdoors. With no harsh shadows and vibrant colors in the sky, it gives your photos a nice warm glow.

How to showcase your space on Airbnb?

There are many ways for you to stand out and display your property in the best possible way. Here are some tips that will help you improve your Airbnb listing's photo section:

Tell a story

Often, people will go through your photos one at a time using the gallery function. This means that they will likely view each photo in the sequence. This gives you the perfect opportunity to tell your property's story in your way.

You can start with a shot of the outside area or the photo you think best represents your space. Then slowly take your profile visitors through the property as if you were giving them a tour in-person. Help them picture how one photo leads to another.

Select the main photo for your Airbnb listing

The purpose of the main photo for your Airbnb listing is to stand out and generate clicks to your profile while engaging your audience, making them want to see more of your property. The main photo is perhaps the most critical item of your complete Airbnb listing, as having the wrong main photo will cost you lots of profile clicks and, therefore, bookings. Your main photo should:

1. **Stand out from your competitors:** Look at the main photos of other properties in your area and find a photo from your

property that would easily stand out amongst them; this could be color-wise, composition-wise, or displaying the content.

2. **Unique selling points:** What are the main unique selling points of your home? Choose a photo that hits a specific iconic experience that you can only get at your Airbnb home. For instance, a photo of the balcony of your Paris apartment overlooking the Eiffel tower, an overflow jacuzzi overlooking a beautiful coastline in Bali, or an exterior photo of your jungle treehouse with vines in Costa Rica. If your property doesn't have views or a well-maintained garden, go with a beautiful shot from the inside! Avoid a photo of just the bed or a single object. It should be a complete overlook of your place (from the best angle) or its best feature or room.

3. **High quality:** Ensure your main photo is bright and high resolution.

Select your top 5 photos

When opening an Airbnb profile on a mobile phone, you'll see one photo. When opening an Airbnb profile on a laptop, you'll see five photos. Therefore, your first five photos should be your best photos.

How many photos you should upload

Depending on your space's size, it is best to have anywhere between 20 to 60 photos in your Airbnb listing. If you rent an 8-bedroom villa, ensure to have photos of all bedrooms, bathrooms, and other details. You'll easily reach the 60 photos. Please keep in mind that it is not about the number of photos, but about the quality and completeness to show your home the right way. Only add photos that genuinely add value to your listing.

Captions

When uploading your photos, Airbnb has the option to add captions to them with a maximum of 250 characters each. Take advantage of this opportunity, and write about facts that aren't immediately obvious. Describe the experience, not the features. Example: Enjoy the romantic sunsets from your private balcony with a good glass of local wine in hand. The first bottle is on us!

Advanced tips

Do you have fast WIFI? Upload a photo of your high-speed WIFI network by doing a speed test and adding a screenshot of the results.

Floorplan

Display the layout of your house by creating a floorplan.

Nearby highlights

Do you have a highlight in the area that is very close to your property? Add screenshots of Google Maps showing the location of your space and the directions to the nearest highlights.

Reviews

Add screenshots of some of your best reviews. This will help to build trust and convince a potential guest to book your property.

Compositions

Do you find it challenging to photograph smaller spaces like bathrooms and hallways in landscape mode? You could create these photos in a portrait mode and then put them together by creating a composition of two portrait photos next to each other, thereby forming a combined landscape photo.

Text or notes

Add text or notes to your photos to clarify a photo. For instance, when taking a picture of the view out of the bedroom window by night. You could add with a simple photo editing tool such as Paint, or even with PowerPoint in the top right corner of the photo in text: Actual view of the bedroom by night.

How to edit your photos?

Have you ever wondered how a real estate photographer can capture such fantastic property exterior photos that look so breathtaking and magical because of perfect lightning? There's a high chance that those photographers used photo editing software to refine and polish their photos.

What is photo editing software? It's an essential part of a digital photographer's process. This is where you edit your photos to balance hues, create special effects, improve saturation, remove blemishes, and more. You can enhance and alternate your photos using photo editing software or the Airbnb photo editor tool.

Important note: Before getting started with editing, backup all original images.

The Airbnb photo editor app

The Airbnb photo editing app is good enough for basic photo editing, such as straightening your photos, increasing brightness. You don't need to apply filters to change the look of your property completely. The Airbnb photo editing app will make your photos look more professional. These are the adjustments you can make with the Airbnb online photo editing tool:

- **Crop:** Remove distracting objects from the focal point.
- **Rotate:** Level the horizon line in your photos.
- **Exposure / Brightness:** Use this if a photo looks too dim or too bright.
- **Contrast:** Brightens lighter areas and darkens others.
- **Airbnb Filter:** A predefined optimal setting by Airbnb.

I have tested the Airbnb photo editing tool on some photos that haven't been made by a professional photographer or have not been post-processed. For some photos, it worked perfectly well. I could increase the brightness, crop, and rotate and have my photos look much better. Test it yourself and see how it works for your photos. You can find the Airbnb photo editing tool here:

1. Go to your listing under your hosting profile and choose the "Edit" option in the photo section.

2. Click on a photo that you wish to edit or enhance.

3. Click on the "Edit" pencil at the bottom right of the photo on the next screen.

4. At the bottom of the next screen, you will see the three options to edit or enhance your image.

5. Rotate, edit, or crop your photo when needed.

6. Click on "Save and Replace" to save your changes.

Professional photo editing software

If the Airbnb photo editing tool isn't enough, then you might need professional photo editing software. These are some of your best options:

- **Adobe Photoshop:** This is the perfect photo editing software for an intermediate or professional photographer. It contains all the tools to edit photos to the highest quality and is the world's industry-standard in photo editing software.

- **Adobe Lightroom:** This powerful photo editor software has become the standard tool for both professionals and beginning photographers. You can adjust the color, exposure, and tonality of a digital image. However, it is limited and not as powerful as Adobe Photoshop in terms of image manipulation, removing spots, changing colors, or composting it with other images.

Have you applied most of the photo recommendations? Congratulations, your photos should now be in the top 20% of all Airbnb listing photos.

Rooms and spaces

To find the "Rooms and spaces" tab in Airbnb, log in to your Airbnb account on a computer, select "Manage listing(s)," open your listing, click on "Listing details," and open the "Rooms and spaces" tab.

In this tab, you can add or edit areas guests can use and mark any spaces they'll share. It is a simple list you should fill out completely:

- Select the type of beds each bedroom has.
- Select if each bedroom comes with a private ensuite bathroom.
- Select at each space if it is shared with others. This could be with you, other guests (these are guests that aren't part of the same reservation), or someone else.
- Assign the photos you have uploaded in Airbnb to each one of the spaces you have marked as available to guests. Attach as many photos as you can to all your spaces. Airbnb might use these to show your listing in a better way to your audience.

Amenities

Here, you can find a selection of amenities Airbnb can publish on your listing profile. According to Airbnb's consumer survey, an overwhelming 97% of US travelers surveyed said amenities impacted their travel experience. Amenities do matter: and Airbnb has revealed what amenities travelers value most. First, Airbnb strongly encourages hosts to provide the following essential amenities in all their listings:

- Toilet paper
- Soap (for hands and body)
- One towel per guest
- One pillow per guest
- Linens for each guest bed

Second, many other items can enhance the guest experience and elevate it from a regular stay to a memorable stay. It is always advisable to throw in a few wow-factor extras. Guests love unique elements and little touches, and it all makes for a more memorable stay.

Research by Airbnb has shown that some of the most sought-after Airbnb amenities are:

- Properties with a Pool
- Pet-friendly properties
- Properties with a kitchen
- Properties that come with free parking

What amenities should you offer at your property? At the "Amenities" tab in your Airbnb profile, you can select all checkboxes for amenities your property has. Try to have as many amenities as possible, but only if they are relevant to your target audience:

- The more valuable amenities you have, the more reasons guest have to stay at your property.
- Some amenities positively influence your Airbnb ranking.
- It helps guests that search with a selection of specific amenities; for instance, guests selecting a kitchen, washer, or dryer to find your home in their search. Therefore, it increases your Airbnb profile visibility.
- If there are some amenities you don't have, try to get them if you think they might be relevant to your target audience. Suppose you have a small studio in a financial district, perfect for business travelers. In that case, having family-friendly amenities is most likely no priority for your Airbnb listing. Therefore choose your extras wisely.

Accessibility

To find the "Accessibility" tab in Airbnb, log in to your Airbnb account on a computer, select "Manage listing(s)," open your listing, click on "Listing details," and select the "Accessibility" tab.

In the accessibility section of your Airbnb profile, you can select the accessibility features that your home comes with, such as having a wheelchair-friendly home. Guests with a mobility need often rely on photos to make sure a listing will work for them. That's why Airbnb requires hosts to provide photos of every accessibility feature they have, and it is why listings have a special section dedicated to showcasing these photos. Making your home accessibility friendly will help you get more reservations as there are only a select number of accessibility-friendly listings on Airbnb. Also, Airbnb is improving the search features, including new filters to find accessibility friendly listings.

We recently decided to add a wheelchair-friendly apartment, as we have received several inquiries in the past from guests looking for a wheelchair-friendly place to stay. Always listen to your guests and write down what amenities or services they would like to have. Perhaps you can easily add them.

Title & description

To find the "Title & description" section in Airbnb, log in to your Airbnb account on a computer, select "Manage listing(s)," open your listing, click on "Listing details," and scroll down until the "Title & description" section.

In the "Title & description" section, you can create your Airbnb title and description to help guests get an idea of what it'll be like to stay in your property.

Internal name

Only you will see the internal name; guests won't see this. This is a helpful feature for hosts with multiple properties to name their properties to identify them quickly.

Listing title

After your main photo, your listing title is your second most important listing feature. A catchy Airbnb title is essential if you want to encourage potential guests to click on your Airbnb listing and explore it in more detail. Your title has 50 characters; use them wisely. I drew a list of options that will help you create an engaging and optimized title that will help you attract visitors to your Airbnb profile:

- **Use all characters:** Airbnb allows up to 50 characters in a title. Try to use as many characters as you can. This should have a positive effect on your ranking and the number of clicks to your profile.

- **Add your location:** Be specific about your property location and include the name of a tourist site or attraction close to your property (only do this if this tourist site attracts lots of travelers to your area). You can also add other location details that your target guests might find appealing.

- **Avoid abstract adjectives:** Such as "good," "nice," or "unique." Instead, go for words that have real meaning, for example, "private," "spacious," or "modern." Mention your unique selling points in your title. If you provide a free parking spot in the center of Paris, don't hesitate to include it in your listing title (this is one of the most frequently searched for amenities). Not sure what the best features are? Read the reviews left by your guests to see what they especially like about your property.

- **Add the number of bedrooms:** Do you have two or more bedrooms? Make this immediately clear for prospective guests. Often, families of three or more struggle to find a property with multiple bedrooms, as studios and one-bedroom apartments are shown more frequently in Airbnb search results. Not everyone uses the search filters. Mention the number of bedrooms in your Airbnb title; this will help win the attention of families and people traveling in groups instantly.

- **Appeal to your target audience**: Let them know you are ready to cater to their needs. Is your property kids-friendly, pets-friendly, or ideal for couples? Use the title to let guests know what you have to offer.

- **Add special characters:** Stand out from other Airbnb listings, using, for instance, the following characters in your title: @, #, ★, ‼, etc. This trick will help to grab guests' attention immediately.

- **Update your title occasionally:** Make your Airbnb listing title relevant to upcoming local events or showcase special offers.

- **Use capital letters**: Draw more attention to your titles, use only capital letters, or mix them. **Important note:** Some guests might find it a bit aggressive to only use capital letters. But would that be a reason for them not to book your property? I doubt it. Using capital letters does get you better visibility in the search and, therefore, possibly more bookings.

- **Add a star rating.** If your property truly is a 5-star property, add it in the title - it can get you extra bookings. However, be careful because you are setting yourself up for big expectations, so you'd better ensure that the guest is satisfied. If not, the chances are high that you'll be rewarded with a bad review.

- **Put the most important first.** Your title might be cut in the Airbnb search, depending on the device the guest is using. Therefore, always put the most important words first.

Title Example:

$60 ⚡ 🏅 ☆ Comfortable Apartment in The City with Gym

$249 ⚡ 🏅 ★★★★★ | TOP LUXURY 2 BEDROOM SUITE | GYM & CINEMA

Listing 1.   Listing 2.

What listing title do you think will generate more clicks? You're right - listing title 2! This is why listing 2 has a strong title:

- Title 2 gets more attention due to using capital letters and starting with special characters: ★★★★★.

- Instead of using words that don't have a value, such as "with" or "in." Vertical lines | and & signs have been used to separate words. These signs save on characters and will also help draw more attention to your title.

- Listing title 2 mentions the number of bedrooms, which can also result in more clicks.

- Listing title 2 says "top luxury." This suggests that this property is not your average Airbnb home; this should attract attention and make Airbnb guests interested in learning more.

- This listing title shows a great unique selling point - the fact that it comes with a cinema. If just a few properties in the area offer a feature that your property has and guests will love it, then it might be worth mentioning in the title.

This is why listing title 1 doesn't have a strong title:

- Listing title 1 says, "comfortable apartment." What does this mean? Should an apartment not always be comfortable?
- Title 1 says, "in the city." This also doesn't mean a lot, especially knowing that to find a property, you'll have to search for a destination, so when searching for a destination, you'll most likely know if this is a city not. Perhaps it would be better if it would say "in the city center."
- Title 1 uses words that don't add any value in the title, such as 'in,' 'the' or 'with.' An Airbnb title only has 50 characters; don't waste them on words that don't add instant value.
- By not using exclusively capital letters, the title doesn't get as much attention as the title of listing 2.
- Additionally, did you notice that the profile picture doesn't fit well, leaving two grey banners on the side? Always ensure that your photo fits perfectly, and if not, crop it.

When it comes to your Airbnb title: get creative, to the point, keep it real, focus on unique selling points, and try to get as many clicks as possible from guests that want to learn more about your property. It is all about converting those viewers into bookers.

Description

Every Airbnb listing comes with seven unique text boxes that you can use to write about your listing. Most importantly, use them all! Only 30% of Airbnb hosts use all the available description boxes. This is an excellent opportunity for you to gain a competitive advantage and distinguish yourself from your competition. Having a 100% completed profile will help you improve your ranking; it will result in more profile visitors and convert more of your listing visitors into bookers (when displaying the right information). This is how you can take full advantage of your listing descriptions:

1. Listing description

Your listing description (also known as the summary) is the first, and therefore most crucial description tab. It shows up on top of your profile when someone visits your profile. This summary description should help guests imagine what it's like to stay at your place and convince them to book. You'll have 500 Characters, so choose your words carefully. Sell your property the right way by applying the following to your summary:

- **Focus on your target audience:** Keep your target audience at the back of your mind and highlight the features that are of the highest importance to them. For example, if you are looking for more reservations from business travelers, mention a comfortable workspace and strong WIFI.
- **Use all 500 characters:** To take full advantage of the number of characters, instead of writing complete text, I use bullet

points to write down as many unique selling points in this summary.

- **Highlight the most important words:** I highlight the most important words by writing them in capital letters.
- **Size or floor level:** Write about your property's size or on what floor level it is located. (important: only do this if it is in your favor; for instance, leave it out if you think your property is small)
- **Unique selling points:** Write about your home's unique selling points, such as the balcony, rooftop, garden, private pool, or barbecue facilities.
- **Onside facilities:** Write about onsite facilities such as a shared gym, private parking, or 24/7 security.
- **Location:** Explain in your summary why your property location is excellent.
- **Mention highlights:** Close to what highlights is your listing located? And how long of a walk or drive does it take to get there?
- **Free stuff:** Do guests get any free stuff? Write about it!
- **Technology:** Write about technology. Do you have fast WIFI, tons of TV channels, a smart speaker, or perhaps a smart lock that allows 24/7 self-check-in?
- **Essential details:** Do you have a washer/dryer onsite? A Fully equipped kitchen? King Size beds? Or ambient lighting? Write about it.

Did you apply the above to your summary? By now, you should have around 500 characters and a compelling listing summary.

Bonus: With this, I share one of my listing summaries that's close to 500 characters. With great success, we applied this example summary styling to some of our best performing listings:

- Brand new SPACIOUS 2 BEDROOM APARTMENT - 142 M2 (1528 sq. ft)
- Shared ROOFTOP Terrace, GYM, KIDS PLAYGROUND & CINEMA
- HIGH-SPEED Internet - 50 Mbps
- 2 FREE private indoor parking spots
- XL Smart TVs with 1000+ Movies & TV Channels
- Washer and dryer IN UNIT
- GREAT downtown location
- 24/7 Reception
- DESIGNER furniture
- Two BALCONIES + Great views
- DINING AREA for 8 guests
- Fully Equipped LUXURY kitchen
- PREMIUM King beds
- BOSE sound system
- AMBIENT Lighting

Import note: If you prefer to write an engaging summary instead of using bullet points, that is completely fine. We do so for some of our listings that have fewer features. For those listings, we often write about how guests would feel inside the property or surroundings instead of feature selling.

2. The space

This description box is the place where you should get into detail about your listing. Give more information about what makes your property unique. You'll have more than enough characters in this description box. Go into detail for each one of the spaces your listing offers. However, don't overdo it, as no-one is looking to read an essay about your property. Keep it simple, honest, and engaging. It is recommendable to:

1. **Focus on your audience:** Keep your target audience at the forefront of your mind and highlight the features that are of the highest importance to them. For example, if you are looking for more reservations from business travelers, mention a comfortable workspace and strong Wi-Fi.
2. **Structure your text**: Divide your text into sections and make it sound friendly — use subheadings and bullet points.
3. **Introduction:** Start with a short introduction about your space, giving more detailed information about the information you have displayed in your summary.
4. **Provide details about all guest spaces:** Continue by creating separate subheadings to provide more information about the bedroom, bathroom, living room, kitchen, and perhaps building or garden. Write about what amenities your fully

equipped kitchen comes with, important bedroom details, and explain your living room layout.

3. Guest access

Let guests know what parts of the space they'll be able to access. If you rent a private home, it might be evident that you have access to the complete house. However, it is still essential to clarify this, as there are many Airbnb Listings with exceptions. Additional ly, write about services your guests have access to outside of the property, such as a gym, pool, garden, tennis court, etc.

4. Guest interaction

Tell guests if you'll be available to offer help throughout their stay and select one of the appropriate options that apply to your Airbnb listing:

1. I plan to socialize with my guests.
2. I give my guests space, but I am available when needed.
3. I won't be available in person.

Additionally, explain in the description text of this section how exactly you are available to guests. Tell them what kind of things you can help with and for what kind of questions they can reach out to you. Take advantage of this description box and show why you are a great host because of the help you can offer to guests, such as organizing transportation, activities, recommendations, restaurant reservations, etc. In our listing profiles, we encourage people to reach out for suggestions, questions, etc. This might sound scary, as you possibly don't want to be your guests' private concierge during their stay. However, in the end, only a small percentage of guests will reach out for recommendations.

5. Neighborhood overview

The neighborhood information is displayed at the bottom of your listing profile. To find this information, a visitor to your profile needs to click on "More about the location." Keep it short but engaging, avoid long lists of activities the guest can do, and instead highlight the top 5 most important activities and things representing your area and where your targeted guests might be looking for.

Let guests know what your neighborhood is like and what makes it unique. For instance, write about that great restaurant around the corner that prepares delicious breakfasts. Mention the highlights guests should visit, and mention the distance in minutes walking or driving to each of these highlights. It is recommendable to use bullet points in this section to make it easy for guests to read.

6. Getting around

Let guests know in this section if your listing is close to public transportation (or far from it). You can also mention nearby parking options - is Uber available or any other taxi services? This is a great spot to add some Uber or Lyft referral codes so that guests get a discount when signing up and you get a commission or travel credit.

You could also use this section for telling guests the distance to the nearest airports, as this is a frequently asked question.

7. Other things to note

Let guests know if other details will impact their stay. This is where you use the text box to write about any other essential features, amenities, or services. Possibly you could also use it to highlight important rules and restrictions. When writing about rules and restrictions, you should, first, use the "House Rules" tab. Only if a rule or regulation is so vital that it should be displayed on your listing page, then this text box is the place to write it down. But be very careful as you don't want to scare away potential guests.

Guests who made it up to this part of your listing are highly interested because they wouldn't have taken all the time to read until here if they weren't. Therefore, add a call to action. Ask the guest to add your property to their wishlist and ask them to reach out for any questions they might have.

Filled out all the seven description boxes? Congrats, you are now one step closer to creating a successful Airbnb listing.

Custom link

> *To find the "Custom link" tab in Airbnb, log in to your Airbnb account on a computer, select "Manage listing(s)," open your listing, click on "Listing details," and open the "Custom link" tab.*

Airbnb now has the option for most Airbnb listings to add a custom link. This is a free feature you should be using, even if you already have a personal website for your property.

Every Airbnb listing comes with a standard URL (stands for Uniform Resource Locator and is used to specify addresses on the World Wide Web) that looks like this: www.airbnb.com/rooms/10654302. As you can see, this URL filled up with numbers isn't very inspiring. Therefore, Airbnb offers hosts the option of creating a memorable and unique URL. This makes your URL look more professional when including your listing on business cards, websites, or social media. Example:

- Before: www.airbnb.com/rooms/10654302
- After:www.airbnb.com/h/luxury-2-bedroom-apartment-new-york

Important note: Opponents of Airbnb's custom URL criticize some of its features. The opportunity seems to be unreliable. The existence of this link depends on Airbnb policies, which means Airbnb can suspend it for any reason if Airbnb decides to discontinue it. Currently, the custom Airbnb link does not affect ranking on search engines. When someone clicks on a custom Airbnb link, they are redirected to the main URL for your Airbnb listing.

Property and guests

> *To find the "Property and Guests" section in Airbnb, log in to your Airbnb account on a computer, select "Manage listing(s)," open your listing, click on "Listing details," and scroll down to the "Property and guests" section.*

In the "Property and guests" section, you'll have to provide more details about the type of property or space you are hosting, and whether it is shared or not:

- What kind of space do you offer
- What is the property type
- Is it an entire place, private room, or shared space
- How many guests can stay in your space
- Does it have a dedicated guest space

Ensure that this information is up to date, as it is crucial for guests to fully understand what type of place you are offering and how many people can stay in it.

Location

To find the "Location" section in Airbnb, log in to your Airbnb account on a computer, select "Manage listing(s)," open your listing, click on "Listing details," and scroll down to the "Location" section.

In this section, you can double-check if your listing address is showing correctly, add instructions to arrive at your property easily, and check if the pin on the map is marking the correct location.

Map marker

Guests with confirmed reservations can always see your listing's exact location and address. However, you can choose how your listing's location will be shown to anyone visiting your listing profile. These are your options:

- **General location:** Before booking your property, Airbnb shows the general area of your listing to guests searching for a place to stay, but not the exact location. Guests can see your listing's neighborhood and how close it is to important landmarks, transportation stops, and other points of interest. After their reservation is confirmed, Airbnb will show them your exact location and address.

- **Specific location:** Airbnb will show a more specific location of your listing to guests searching for a place to stay. Guests will see a small circular pin that shows your listing location with greater accuracy, but not the exact point. Airbnb still shows your exact location and address to guests with confirmed reservations.

Showing the exact location should result in more reservations, as most guests like to know where exactly they'll be staying. For security reasons, you might choose to go for the 'general location' option; just take in mind that in this case, you will most likely get plenty of guests asking for the exact location. If this happens, you can always, in a friendly way, explain to a potential guest that, for security reasons, the precise location of your listing will only be provided once a reservation is confirmed.

Directions

In the directions text box, you can fill out the exact address to your listing, add - for instance - the Google Maps link, share directions to your place, public transportation options, and parking tips. Keep it short and engaging.

Important note: For additional privacy. There is a checkbox at the end of this Airbnb section asking if you'd like Airbnb not to share your address, last name, or phone number while guests can still cancel for free. After the free cancellation window, the guest will receive this information. This option gives you additional privacy but can make it harder for guests to plan their trip. Therefore, it is recommendable not to mark this option, only do so if it is essential.

Things your guests should know

To find the "Things your guests should know" tab in Airbnb, log in to your Airbnb account on a computer, select "Manage listing(s)," open your listing, click on "Listing details," and open the "Things your guests should know" tab.

This section of your Airbnb profile covers questions a guest may have before they're ready to book – and helps avoid surprises later on, such as:

- **Safety Considerations:** Are there any safety considerations at or around your property that guests should be aware of?
- **Safety Devices:** Does your property have any safety devices such as a carbon monoxide alarm or smoke alarm?
- **Property Info:** Any limitations or essential details your guests should know about, such as the potential for noise, pets at the property, or amenity limitations?

Ensure that you read the options carefully in Airbnb. To complete this section, simply mark each one of the checkboxes displayed. This will help improve your guest expectations and should have a positive result on your guests' satisfaction and review scores.

Guest resources

To find the "Guest resources" section in Airbnb, log in to your Airbnb account on a computer, select "Manage listing(s)," open your listing, click on "Listing details," and scroll down to the "Guest resources" section.

The information displayed in the guest's resources section is only available for guests who have confirmed their reservation at your Airbnb listing. Here, you can add information such as:

- **Check-in instructions:** Select the type of check-in service you offer at your listing, and fill out any vital information in the textbox that comes with it.
- **WIFI details:** What is your WIFI name and password? This is one of the most frequently asked questions from guests. Fill out your WIFI details in this Airbnb section to ensure that guests get connected easily. Guests receive the WIFI details in their reservation confirmation. Also, place a printed WIFI details sign inside your property.
- **House manual:** Your house manual should contain tips, instructions, rules, and the answers to frequently asked questions about your property. For instance: how to access the internet? Or how to turn on the hot water? Anything that guests often ask. But desist from writing too much information as guests would most likely not read it all. Use bullet points, subheadings, and clear and engaging writing.

Guidebook

> *To find the "Guidebook" tab in Airbnb, log in to your Airbnb account on a computer, select "Manage listing(s)" open your listing, click on "Listing details," and open the "Guidebook" tab.*

In the "Guidebook" tab, you can create your customized Airbnb guidebook. Hosts with guidebooks tend to get more bookings—win over potential guests with yours. Guidebooks let hosts suggest local spots, like restaurants, grocery stores, parks, and attractions. Some cities also have city guidebooks, which are combined lists of recommendations that hosts have added to their guidebooks.

It is recommendable to create your personalized local guidebook. It will help you increase visibility and save you time, as guests can use your guidebook instead of asking you questions. Add your recommendations in your Airbnb guidebook for:

- **Places:** What places should your guests visit?
- **Neighborhoods:** What neighborhoods or areas should they visit?
- **Advice**: What important thing should your guests know about your area?

You can write about anything that might add value to your guests. Identify first where they might be interested in and add that to your guidebook; for instance, restaurant recommendations, highlights, or essential advice, for example, whether it is recommendable to drink tap water.

Expert tip: Do you have several properties within the same area? You can create one guidebook for several listings in the same area. Just add your photos and descriptions once and then select to show your guidebook at your other relevant listings.

Booking settings

In your Airbnb listings' booking setting, you can update anything from policies to house rules, guest requirements, and more. Choosing the right booking settings is essential to your success on Airbnb.

How guests can book

To find the "How guests can book" tab in Airbnb, log in to your Airbnb account on a computer, select "Manage listing(s)," open your listing, click on "Booking Settings," and open the "How guests can book" tab.

In the "How guests can book" tab, you can choose how guests will book your home. You have two options:

1. **Instant bookings:** Guests who meet all your requirements can book instantly. Others will need to send a reservation request. You can cancel 100% penalty-free if you're ever uncomfortable with a reservation.
2. **Reservation requests:** All guests must send a reservation request.

Instant Book listings don't require approval from the host to get booked. Instead, guests can just choose their travel dates, book, and then discuss check-in plans with the host after confirmation. If you have the Instant Book functionality on, it will automatically apply to all available dates on your calendar. Guests who meet your requirements will be able to book your space instantly. According to Airbnb, the benefits of Instant Book include:

- **Convenience**: Guests confirm their reservation without having to talk to you first.
- **Increased guest interest**: Guests can use a specific search filter to search for listings that can be booked instantly. Instant Book listings are more popular with guests since it allows them to plan their trip more efficiently.
- **Search placement**: Accepting instantly booked reservations positively affects your listing's response rate, and therefore improves your listing's position in search results.
- **Superhost status**: Instant book can help you reach Superhost status more easily, as this requires you to maintain a minimum 90% response rate.

Important note: When having the instant book option activated, your calendar should always be up to date. You don't want to have to tell a guest that their booked dates aren't available. Having to cancel a guest reservation that is already confirmed will result in the following penalties:

1. **Host cancellations:**
    a. As a host, if you cancel a guest reservation more than seven days before check-in, Airbnb will deduct $50 from your next payout.

b. As a host, if you cancel a guest reservation less than seven days before check-in, Airbnb will deduct $100 from your next payout.

c. The cancellation fee may be waived if you have completed at least ten consecutive bookings without cancelling, either since you started hosting or since your last cancellation.

2. **Unavailable/blocked calendar:** Your calendar will stay blocked, and you won't be able to accept another reservation for the same dates as the canceled reservation through Airbnb.

3. **Lower-ranking:** Airbnb penalizes the ranking of properties that have host cancellations.

4. **Cancellation review:** Airbnb will leave a review on your listing to indicate that the host canceled the reservation. This might hurt future reservations because many guests don't like to book with a host, knowing that their reservation might get canceled.

5. **Account suspension.** If you cancel three or more reservations within a year, Airbnb may even deactivate your listing.

6. **Challenging to become a Superhost.** It will be harder for a host that cancels guest reservations to either reach or maintain Superhost status. As an Airbnb Superhost, you are allowed only to cancel less than 1% of your reservations.

When unable to host a reservation, Airbnb will enable you to cancel penalty-free, but only under the following circumstances:

1. **Issues with the guest:** The guest has several unfavorable reviews on their Airbnb profile that concern the host, the guest hasn't responded to questions the host needs to know about their trip, or the guest makes it clear they'll likely break one of the host's house rules, like bringing a pet or smoking.

2. **Death:** If a host, guest, co-host, additional guest, immediate family member, or caregiver passes away. You'll be asked to provide one of these documents:
   a. Death certificate
   b. Obituary
   c. News article naming the deceased
   d. Police report

3. **Illness or injury:** In case of a severe unexpected illness or injury.

4. **Government-mandated obligations:** For instance: jury duty, travel restrictions, or court appearances.

5. **Unforeseen property damage**: These are unexpected damages such as water leakage or gas escape.

6. **Transportation disruptions:** If it is not possible to travel to your property.

7. **Circumstances that require thorough review:** For example, natural disasters, terrorist activity, or epidemic diseases such as the COVID-19 virus.

Important note: It is highly recommendable to have Instant Book activated as it will get you more reservations. If you work with other booking platforms and are afraid of overbookings, consider synchronizing your Airbnb calendar using iCalendar or channel management software to connect to other calendars. I'll explain in detail how to set this up in the "Sync Calendar" tab section.

Guest requirements

To find the "Guest requirements" section in Airbnb, log in to your Airbnb account on a computer, select "Manage listing(s)," open your listing, click on "Booking Settings," and scroll down to the "Guest requirements" section.

In this section, you select how you'd like Airbnb to verify your guests. Every guest that books your Airbnb listing is verified at least in the following ways:

- By their phone number.
- By their email address.
- By their payment information.
- By their agreement to your house rules.
- Additionally, you can require Airbnb to show guests their profile photo once a reservation is confirmed.

If you allow guests to book instantly, you can require in addition to the last points to also:

- Submit their government ID to Airbnb.
- Have recommendations from other Airbnb hosts and no negative reviews.

Important note: The downside of additional verifications is that these are extra steps a guest must take, and in some cases, might withhold guests from booking. Therefore, requesting them might result in fewer reservations for your Airbnb listing.

Pre-booking message

Anything else you'd like your guests to know before confirming their reservation? You can require guests to read and respond to a message with this text box before confirming their reservation. For instance, you could write a pre-booking welcome message or write about the things guests should know in advance.

House rules

To find the "House Rules" section in Airbnb, log in to your Airbnb account on a computer, select "Manage listing(s)," open your listing, click on "Booking Settings," and scroll down to the "House Rules" section.

In the "House Rules" section, you can create and select your preferred house rules. As a host, you should share your house rules to set expectations with your guests, for instance, rules for smokers, what areas guests aren't allowed to use, and permission to have visitors.

House rules appear on your listing page, and guests must review and agree to them before requesting a reservation. They're also sent directly to a guest once they have confirmed their reservation. It is a way of protecting your listing from unwanted guests or activities. Keep your house rules friendly, straightforward, and short. If you don't, guests might be scared away or won't read it all. Select in the house rules section whether your listing is:

- Suitable for children from 2 to 12 years old.
- Suitable for infants under 2 years old.
- If pets are allowed.
- If smoking is allowed.
- If parties and events are allowed.

Most hosts say that pets, smoking, or parties aren't allowed. Take in mind that if you allow these options, you could get a fair share of new reservations simply because there is less supply of hosts allowing them. Additionally, you could clarify your regulations in the house rules description tab. For example:

- Smoking is permitted, but only on the designated outside areas such as on the balcony with the balcony doors closed, rooftop terrace, or in front of the building. Smoking is never allowed indoors.

- Pets are allowed if well trained. We charge an additional fee of $20 per night per pet, and guests are fully responsible for any damage or dirt pets might create.
- Parties and events are allowed. However, only after preapproval of the host – i.e., get in touch and share the event's purpose, how many attendees, and any additional information we should know. Once approved, we'll get back to you with a price quote.

As you can see with the three examples above, I have changed the restrictions into opportunities. This helps to sell more and stand out from the crowd. This is a great way to create a competitive advantage and monetize your listing where possible.

Additional rules

In the last part of the house rules section, you'll find a textbox to write about additional rules. Here you should write your most important rules and regulations in a friendly and transparent way, preferably with bullet points. This is also where you should specify the examples. When staying in some of our homes, we kindly ask guests to accept the following rules:

- Only pre-registered guests have access to the property.
- Please help us save the environment by turning off all the lights and air-conditioners when leaving the property.
- Please do not smoke inside the apartment; smoking is only allowed outside on the balcony.

- As the building is a residential complex with families, couples, and older people, we kindly ask you to keep quiet after 10 PM.

And we finish this text box with the following sentence: Thank you for considering the above when enjoying your stay with us, and please feel free to reach out if there is anything we can do to make your stay more comfortable.

Policies

> *To find the "Policies" section in Airbnb, log in to your Airbnb account on a computer, select "Manage listing(s)," open your listing, click on "Booking Settings," and scroll down to the "Policies" section.*

In the "Policies" section, you can select your favorite check-in/check-out policy and cancellation policy. Choosing the right policies is essential for increasing your Airbnb earnings. Let me explain to you why.

Check-in/check-out policy

If you want to sell as many room nights as you can on Airbnb, you should allow same-day check-ins and check-outs. Enabling this means that you must stay in control of your guest check-ins and check-outs. The last thing you want; is having guests arrive while your home is still occupied, dirty, or being cleaned. Most Airbnb hosts allow guests to check-in around 3-4 PM and check-out around 10 AM to 12 PM to prevent this from happening. This should give most hosts enough time (2-4 hours) to have their space perfectly cleaned and ready for the next guest's arrival. Optimize your check-in/check-out policy the following way:

- **Reasonable time frame:** Choose reasonable check-in and check-out times; for example, check-out at noon and check-in at 3 PM. You might lose potential bookings when offering only late check-ins and very early check-outs.
- **Check-in template:** Add the earliest check-in and latest check-out time for your property in your standard check-in message. Send this message to guests immediately after they have booked your property.
- **Check-out template:** Additionally, one day before check-out, send your guests a 'thank you for your stay' note and the latest check-out time and check-out constructions.
- **Cleaning:** Ensure that cleaners have sufficient time to clean your property. If you feel that they take too long, try to improve their cleaning process or hire a professional cleaner/cleaning company.

Cancellation policy

Choosing the right cancellation policy for your Airbnb listing is essential for your success on the platform. Airbnb wants you to choose a policy that is as flexible as possible, as this will help increase bookings. However, as a host, you'd likely prefer a strict cancellation policy as no host likes to receive last-minute cancellations that are penalty-free, resulting in having your home empty. Therefore, choose your cancellation policy carefully. These are the six Airbnb cancellation policies you can choose from:

1. **Flexible cancellation policy:** With this policy, you allow guests to receive a full refund when cancelling at least one day before arrival.

2. **Flexible or non-refundable cancellation policy:** In addition to your flexible cancellation policy, you'll offer a non-refundable option — guests pay 10% less. Still, you keep your payout no matter when they cancel.

3. **Moderate cancellation policy:** This policy allows guests to receive a full refund when cancelling at least five days before arrival.

4. **Moderate or non-refundable cancellation policy:** In addition to your moderate cancellation policy, you'll offer a non-refundable option — guests pay 10% less. Still, you keep your payout no matter when they cancel.

5. **Strict cancellation policy:** This policy allows a full refund for cancellations made within 48 hours of booking if the check-in date is at least 14 days away. It allows a 50% refund for cancellations made at least seven days before check-in, and no refund for cancellations made within seven days of check-in.

6. **Strict or non-refundable cancellation policy:** In addition to your strict cancellation policy, you'll offer a non-refundable option — guests pay 10% less. Still, you keep your payout no matter when they cancel.

What cancellation policy should you choose

The short answer is, 'that depends on your listing.' Let me explain to you why. Selecting the right cancellation policy for your listing should depend on the number of cancellations your listing receives on average, and how far in advance guests book. If most of your bookings are last minute bookings, then having a strict cancellation policy is not needed for your listing. If, on average, guests book one month or further in advance. And when cancelling within 14 days before the date of arrival, your home will likely stay empty, then having a flexible cancellation policy might hurt your Airbnb earnings instead. Airbnb did a pilot where they saw an increase of 5% earnings for hosts who offered an additional non-refundable policy, even considering that the non-refundable policy has a 10% discount.

We have tried several cancellation policies for our business and haven't seen a considerable increase in bookings for non-refundable or flexible policies. However, when working with the flexible cancellation policy, we did receive quite some cancellations that resulted in having our listings empty without any earnings. We prefer to work with a strict cancellation policy. Primarily due to our commitment to the owners of the properties we work with. Having to tell a business partner that their one-month booking was canceled three days before check-in penalty-free isn't good for the partnership. If you are new to Airbnb or haven't tried the different policies yet, give it a try, set them flexibly, and see how this works for you. If it doesn't work well, put them slightly stricter until you're satisfied with the results.

Pricing

The highest-earning Airbnb hosts have one crucial thing in common when it comes to pricing - They all have an effective dynamic pricing strategy. The ones that don't, leave money on the table.

Nightly price

To find the "Nightly price" tab in Airbnb, log in to your Airbnb account on a computer, select "Manage listing(s)," open your listing, click on "Pricing," and open the "Nightly price" tab.

You can choose your nightly rates in this tab and whether you'd like to update these manually or automatically. There are three ways to update your listing pricing on Airbnb. In this section, I'll show you what strategy works best for you.

1. Update your pricing manually: It is essential to carefully study your market before uploading your Airbnb rates. Take in mind the following data points:

- **Your Airbnb Listing Availability:** How many days do you still have unbooked?
- **Seasonality**: Every destination has its low, mid, and high season.
- **Day of the week:** Find out what days of the week are the highest demanded in your area.

- **Events in your area:** Any large events within the next 24 months that attract travelers to your location?

- **Pricing of similar listings on Airbnb:** Find similar well-performing Airbnb listings, open their calendars, and check their nightly rates + charges.

- **Occupancy of similar listings on Airbnb:** Find out how many bookings that similar listings in your area have, by opening their Airbnb's calendars and verifying whether most last-minute dates are booked or available.

- **Pricing of hotels in your area:** Check the prices of nearby hotels. This is an excellent way to understand the pricing in your area better.

- **Time left to book**: The closer you are to a specific date, the less time you have to sell.

- **Other booking platforms**: Check the prices for similar homes on Booking.com, Expedia, HomeAway, and TripAdvisor.

Have you done the above? Now take in mind the following tips:

- **Upload a low base price:** Airbnb will ask you to upload your base price. Take your standard rate, discount it by 20% and put that discounted rate as your base price. Why? Because this is the rate that often will be shown on your profile when guests search for it without selecting dates. The lower the rate, the more clicks your listing might get. I use it myself too and have seen an increase in bookings. So, where do you upload the rates you'd like your guests to pay? Directly in your calendar. Open your Calendar, select your date ranges, and update your rates for the next 24 months. The rate you'll upload here is the rate guests will pay.

- **New listing offer:** Is your listing new on Airbnb, and doesn't it have reviews yet? Lower your price by 20% to get visibility and get your first reservations. Guests often are a bit hesitant with new listings that don't have reviews. Try to get at least three good reviews as soon as possible, so that your ranking, profile visitors, and conversion rate will increase. You'd better start with prices that might be on the low side. Not getting any reservation because of charging rates that are too high will result in a lower ranking, less visibility, fewer profile visitors, and, therefore, a potential loss of revenue.

- **Price for max earnings:** Don't price your Airbnb listing for max occupancy. Price for max earnings. 100% occupancy at $75 nightly is monthly $75 × 30 Days = $2250. Having an 80% occupancy with a $120 nightly rate is monthly $120 × 24 Days = $2880. This is an increase of $630 in monthly earnings while having a lower occupancy rate, less work, and fewer costs.

Take in mind that you should frequently update your rates to see the best results. For our listings, I do a quick daily pricing update; I update our standard rates once a year, ensuring that I have at least 24 months of availability anytime. Additionally, I update last-minute availability daily up to 1 month in advance. This strategy works very well for us, as some of our listings have over 90% year-round occupancy with higher prices than our competitors.

2. Use the Airbnb smart pricing tool: The Airbnb smart pricing tool will ask you for your lowest and highest rate, add dynamic pricing to it, and it will automatically adjust your price based on demand on an ongoing basis. Your price stays within the range you set, and you can change it at any time. Airbnb smart pricing takes over 70 different factors into account that could influence your nightly price, such as:

- **Market popularity:** If more people are searching for a place to stay in your area, your price will update.
- **Lead-time:** As a check-in date approaches, your price will be updated.
- **Seasonality:** As you move into, or out of high season, your price will update.
- **Listing popularity:** If you get more views and bookings, your price will update.
- **Listing details:** If you add amenities, such as WIFI, your price will update.
- **Bookings history:** Your future prices are partly based on the prices you received for successful bookings in the past. For instance, if you set your price higher than Airbnb's smart pricing suggests and get a successful booking at that price, the algorithm will update to reflect that.
- **Review history:** Your prices update when you get more positive reviews from completed stays.

How does Airbnb's smart pricing tool interact with other pricing settings? Prices guests see, can be adjusted based on some other settings you have in place, for example:

- **Weekend pricing:** If smart pricing is turned on, your weekend price setting will not be used. Still, Airbnb ensures that the recommended price stays above your minimum price setting, including on weekends.
- **Extra fees:** Additional guest fees and cleaning fees are applied to stays in the same way, whether smart pricing is on or off.
- **Long-stay discounts:** Weekly and monthly discounts are applied to your calendar prices for extended stays, whether smart pricing is on or off.
- **Flexibility:** Additionally, Airbnb adds flexibility to smart pricing, such as the ability to turn it off for specific days only.

Sounds like the perfect option, right? Unfortunately, it turns out that Airbnb might have other goals than you. One of the main difficulties with the Airbnb pricing strategy is that Airbnb's smart pricing tool is based on both the guests' and the hosts' needs. This means that it is stuck between keeping the prices low for guests, while trying to make it profitable for the hosts. And as a host, you would want to optimize for profit, not occupancy.

As this is a conflict of interest, this tool might be underpricing your listing to get frequent bookings, and keeping guests happy for booking excellent rates. Also, bear in mind that your property might have a more luxurious decor than your competitor's property. The tool doesn't consider this.

3. Purchase automated pricing software: Do you prefer not to take the time to update your rates manually on Airbnb, and think that Airbnb's pricing tool is lacking functionalities or results? Purchasing automated pricing software might be the perfect solution for you. There are a handful of companies offering automated pricing software for Airbnb.

For our listings, we manually update our pricing on Airbnb. I am a control freak and numbers person; I know our market by heart and only need 5 minutes daily to update our rates. I also adjust the last-minute length of stay restrictions of our listings daily, especially to fill up gaps and better meet the demand. However, this might be different for new hosts or hosts with listings spread around several countries and destinations with unique travel trends.

I'd recommend you to only manually update your rates on Airbnb if you take the time to investigate your market profoundly and will keep track of your property performance daily. If you can't or prefer not to, I'd highly recommend using an external pricing tool or the Airbnb free pricing tool. With the Airbnb pricing tool, you can set your lowest rate on the high-side and your highest rate ridiculously high. This way, you won't have the adverse side effects of Airbnb offering your listing too cheap, and even better, they can only go up with the rate. It also helps you not miss out when that important event is scheduled in your area, and demand suddenly increases. Just verify your calendar frequently and lower your rates when needed. For instance, last minute, so you won't keep your listing empty. You could consider this as being a semi-automated pricing strategy for your listing. If you want to be completely hands off, I'd suggest going with external pricing software.

Important note: Automated pricing companies often charge a fixed monthly fee per listing or a percentage per reservation, so calculate your costs versus the potential increase in earnings. Before you start working with any of these businesses, confirm if they offer their services in your local market, and perhaps try a free trial at first.

Airbnb calendar discounts

> *To create Airbnb calendar discounts, log in to your Airbnb account on a computer, select "Manage listing(s)," and visit your listing calendar.*

When opening your Airbnb listing Calendar, you have two options to create promotions:

1. You can click on any date, select a specific date range, adjust the rate, and save it. This will change the rate, and in most cases, won't give you any additional visibility, such as the new price being highlighted.

2. Or click on the "Promote your listing tab" in your calendar. Select your custom date range

 Promote your listing **New**
A new way to get noticed

or an Airbnb selection of less popular nights for your listing. Select a discount percentage. A promotion created with the "Promote your listing" tab automatically comes with the perks below:

- **1-25% discount:** A new line item on your price breakdown.
- **10-25% discount:** A new line item on your price breakdown, plus a strikethrough styling on search pages and your listing.
- **15-25% discount:** Get everything above, plus a message on your listing page that highlights the deal you are offering.
- **20-25% discount:** Get everything above, plus a spot in the emails Airbnb sends to guests.

I'd recommend you use the promotion tab! Thanks to the perks provided. Creating a promotion with the "Promote your listing" tab will result in more reservations than merely adjusting your calendar rates.

Length-of-stay discounts

To find the "Length-of-stay-discounts" tab in Airbnb, log in to your Airbnb account on a computer, select "Manage listing(s)," open your listing, click on "Pricing," and select the "Length-of-stay discounts" tab.

Important note: This feature doesn't work when you use the Airbnb smart pricing tool. The Airbnb smart pricing tool overrules these length-of-stay discount settings.

In the length-of-stay discount tab, you can set up extended stay discounts. You can discount by the week, month, or a custom timeframe. It is recommendable to take advantage of the weekly and monthly discount options, even if you are willing to offer a 5% discount. According to Airbnb:

- Most guests looking for stays longer than one month actively look for listings with monthly deals.
- Weekly and monthly discounts are visible to guests in search results. A highlighted discounted price displays next to the original price, and on your listing page, which shows a highlighted weekly or monthly discount on the price breakdown before the total.

Loading length-of-stay discount increases your visibility and will result in more reservations. Isn't it every host's dream to only have long-stay reservations?

Early bird discount

To find the "Early bird discount" tab in Airbnb, log in to your Airbnb account on a computer, select "Manage listing(s)," open your listing, click on "Pricing," and select the "Early bird discount" tab.

Important: This feature doesn't work when you use the Airbnb smart pricing tool. The Airbnb smart pricing tool overrules the early bird discount settings.

Offer a discount for bookings that happen well in advance. Choose how many months up to the date of arrival that guests get an additional discount, add the percentage and click on the "Save" button to save your deal. Using the early bird discount should result in more reservations due to the additional visibility and better rates.

Expert tip: How to get the discount pricing visuals without offering a discount? Increase the rates in your calendar with, for instance, 20% for bookings far ahead. And then, create the 20% discount offer with an early bird discount tool. This way, your rate is the same, while it will be shown with the highlighted discounted price tagging displayed next to the original price. Just ensure that you'll re-update your early bird rates correctly, for instance, once a month.

Last-minute discounts

To find the "Last-minute discounts" tab in Airbnb, log in to your Airbnb account on a computer, select "Manage listing(s)," open your listing, click on "Pricing," and open the "Last-minute discounts" tab.

Important: This feature doesn't work when you use the Airbnb smart pricing tool. The Airbnb smart pricing tool overrules these last-minute discount settings.

The last-minute discount section allows you to offer a discount for bookings that happen close to the arrival date. Insert the number of days before arrival the discount should start, and add the discount percentage you'd like to offer.

I am a big fan of using last-minute specials to increase our listings' occupancy and Airbnb earnings. However, I don't use the auto last-minute discount tool for it. I prefer to stay in control and take several factors in mind, such as how many of my other listings within the same building are available last minute. Also, I'd take into consideration weekends/weekdays, seasonality, and local events.

Therefore, I update my discounted last-minute rates directly in my Airbnb calendar manually or with the promote your listing tab. Daily, I look at my multi-calendar (the multi-calendar is available for hosts with several listings). This calendar shows me what listings still have last-minute availability and for what rates. I lower our apartments' rates with price steps of about $10 per day, starting three days ahead. For most of our listings, this works well because the average booking window (the period between the reservation date and the arrival date) is very short.

I have thoroughly tested this discounting process, and the results are fantastic. We have seen a steady increase in earnings. We rent several similar apartments in some buildings, so we lowered some of the listings last-minute, and others we didn't lower. The properties with last-minute discounts received about 25% more reservations, and more importantly, the total monthly earnings were about 15% higher than the listings without last-minute specials.

Standard fees and charges

To find the "Standard fees and charges" tab in Airbnb, log in to your Airbnb account on a computer, select "Manage listing(s)," open your listing, click on "Pricing," and open the "Standard fees and charges" tab

In the "Standard fees and charges" Airbnb tab, you can add several additional fees to your listing, such as a security deposit or cleaning fee. A great way to protect your property or cover specific costs.

The cleaning fee

Every Airbnb listing should have a reasonably priced cleaning fee. Yes, even when you clean your property yourself or even if you don't have cleaning costs! Why?

1. When a guest selects a maximum nightly rate they like to pay, Airbnb, in many cases, does not include the cleaning fee, other fees, and the Airbnb service fee; therefore, your listing will look cheaper at first. When guests check your detailed pricing calculation, they can see a cleaning fee, or other fees that have been added. It is a simple trick to increase clicks to your profile and get more reservations.

2. I'd recommend setting your cleaning fee to your actual cost of cleaning. This gives you flexibility so that if someone wants to book a single night, your cleaning costs are covered.

You're then free to price your nightly rate at whatever makes sense without having to worry about "losing" money because of short stays.

Important note: The cleaning fee is for cleaning the property after a guest checks out. Take in mind that if a guest cancels their booking before arrival, Airbnb will refund the cleaning fee to the guest. Also, don't overprice your cleaning fee, as this might result in fewer bookings and upset guests. Check your competition and ensure that you don't charge more than them. Setting up your cleaning fee the right way will result in more reservations for a higher average nightly rate.

Security deposit

Having a security deposit gives peace of mind, right? For hosts, the security deposit is a sense of security as you want to protect your Airbnb property from any damage or theft. And, in case something happens, ensure that all the costs involved are covered.

It's the quickest way for you to receive money in the event damage occurs. More may flow from other sources, such as the Host Guarantee Policy, but the payouts from these sources might take weeks. You'll often need capital quickly as repairs need to be completed as soon as possible before the next guest arrives. In case you'd like to use the security deposit, initiate the claims process with the Airbnb Resolution Center: www.airbnb.com/resolutions. Airbnb has two types of security deposits:

1. **Host-required security deposits**: A host-required security deposit can be set between $100 and $5,000. Guests don't pay this deposit when they book a property. They will only be charged if a host submits a claim through the Airbnb Resolution Center. Depending on the damage, the amount the host requests may or may not be the same as the security deposit. If the claim is higher, hosts can apply for the Host Guarantee program that provides property damage protection of up to. With this program, hosts are required to provide documentation of the damaged or missing items and request reimbursement from the guest through the Resolution Center within 14 days of check-out or before the next guest checks in (whichever is earlier). If the guest is unwilling or unable to reimburse, the host can involve Airbnb. Airbnb security deposits must be handled through Airbnb. They can't be paid in cash or through any other off-site payment method.

2. **Airbnb-required security deposits:** For some reservations, Airbnb may independently require a security deposit. In this case, a hold will be placed on the cardholder's cart. If no property damage occurs during the guests' stay, a release of the funds will be provided on their card 14 days after checkout, or before the next guest checks-in. This a great feature that most hosts don't know. It works automatically, and you don't have to opt-in or opt-out for it.

Taking the above into consideration, having a Host-required security deposit should be a no-brainer for your business. Your guest won't be charged for it, and you are better covered for damages, theft, and other incidents. It is recommendable that the security deposit shouldn't exceed more than 20% of a booking's total cost. On average, hosts are charging a security deposit between $100-$500 per reservation. The guest will see what security deposit is charged before booking; therefore, keep it reasonable; you don't want to scare your guests off.

Extra guest fees

Most Airbnb hosts with small listings will charge a fixed price per night, not taking any extra guest charges in mind. However, charging for additional guests might be an attractive extra source of income.

Does your property have a sofa bed in the living room or several bedrooms? Charging an extra fee per guest will help you cover the increase in costs when additional guests stay over, such as water, electricity, gas, and cleaning costs. It will also ensure that your pricing is more attractive for smaller groups.

However, additional guest fees might also come with some challenges. For instance, not every guest might be honest about the total number of guests staying at your property.

When choosing the right price for additional guests, it is essential to consider that being too expensive will result in not getting booked. As a thumb rule, you can charge extra guests 50% of the regular costs per guest.

Example: Catherine has a one-bedroom apartment listed on Airbnb with space for two guests in the bedroom and two guests on the sofa bed in the living room. She charges $100 nightly on Airbnb for two guests. Applying the thumb rule discussed above, her guests pay $50 per person with a standard occupancy of 2 guests. Therefore, it is recommendable to charge the extra 3rd and 4th guests: 50% × $50 = $25 per person per night extra to use the sofa bed. This rate is reasonable and will help you to increase your Airbnb earnings.

Weekend pricing

Important note: this feature doesn't work when you use the Airbnb smart pricing tool. The Airbnb smart pricing tool overrules the weekend price settings.

In the weekend pricing section, you can insert your base price for every Friday and Saturday night. Depending on your destination, you have the following options:

1. **Increase:** Is your property located in an area with more demand on the weekends than during the week? For instance, because of weekend tourism, which often is the case in big cities, beach destinations, etc. Then try to increase your rate a bit from Friday to Sunday, e.g., start with a 20% price increase and see if your guests keep on booking. If they don't, lower your rates last minute with Airbnb's "promote your listing tool."

2. **Decrease:** Decrease your nightly rate at weekends. Is your listing located in a business district with little tourism? Then it might be better to offer a slightly cheaper rate on the weekends.

3. **Leave it untouched:** If not relevant to your market, leave it untouched.

Other standard fees:

To cover additional costs that come with your bookings, Airbnb offers the following other fee options:

- Resort fee
- Management fee
- Community fee
- Linen fee

Import note: To not create a massive list of fees (as this will likely scare your guests off), this is how standard fees are applied: The linens fee is added to the cleaning fee. All other fees are included in the nightly price for guests when they book. You'll get a full rate breakdown in your payout report. In short words, the guest will only see a cleaning fee and your standard rate (which will include all other fees).

Sharing settings

To find the "Sharing settings" tab in Airbnb, log in to your Airbnb account on a computer, select "Manage listing(s)," open your listing, click on "Pricing," and select the "Sharing settings" tab.

In the "Sharing settings" tab, you can select what other hosts will see about your listing and what you will see about other listings. Guests compare everything from house rules to reviews, but pricing is one of the top reasons for choosing a place. To better understand your competition, Airbnb has a tool that allows you to learn more about the listings that your potential guests are also interested in. If you share some details about your listing, you can, in return, see the listings that guests end up booking after seeing your Airbnb listing.

When it comes to sharing settings, Airbnb offers three different options to hosts:

1. **Share listing and booking details:** You'll see the listing titles and photos and the booking details (booked prices, dates, and number of guests). Other hosts will get this same information from you.

2. **Share booking details (default setting):** You'll see the booking details (booked prices, dates, and number of guests), but not the listing titles and photos. Other hosts will get to see either your listing details or your booking details, but not both at the same time.

3. **None:** You won't see or share any information.

Expert tip: If you are struggling to find the right pricing for your listing, then I suggest you leave this tool on for a while, selecting option 1. The tool will help you understand what guests are booking in your area, and you'll know better who your competition is. However, your competition will get the same information about your listing. If you feel you have your pricing strategy under control and bookings are coming in, turn this feature off again to ensure that other hosts won't take advantage of your pricing strategy.

Currency

To find the "Currency" tab in Airbnb, log in to your Airbnb account on a computer, select "Manage listing(s)," open your listing, click on "Pricing," and select the "Currency" tab.

The currency you select in this tab will be the currency used in your Airbnb Calendar. If your country's currency isn't listed here, choose the currency most of your guests will use. For instance, when most of your guests are from the USA, set your calendar currency in US dollars. This will make it easier to create psychological pricing, known as the practice of setting prices slightly lower than a whole number. An example of psychological Airbnb pricing is setting your listing price at $99 rather than $100. This type of pricing has proven to generate more sales. If the guest is using another currency, the pricing will be adjusted according to the daily currency exchange rate, and therefore, will show different numbers. Guests can book with many foreign currencies; however, you will always be paid in your preferred selected payout currency.

The Airbnb service fee

There is a significant difference between the price you upload in your calendar, the price Airbnb pays you per reservation, and the price your guests are being charged by Airbnb for their reservation. This is due to the Airbnb service fees. According to Airbnb, these services fees help run their business smoothly and cover the costs of Airbnb's products and services, like 24/7 customer support.

Fees for booking a place to stay

Airbnb has two different service fee structures for booking a place to stay: a shared host and guest fee, and a host-only fee. The shared host and guest fee has been the standard fee structure at Airbnb for many years. However, recently, Airbnb is stepping away from this model, making it mandatory for many hosts to charge the host-only fee exclusively.

1. Shared host and guest fee: The shared host and guest fee is a fee structure where Airbnb charges both the guest and the host.

- **Host service fee:** This fee is 3% for most hosts, but may be higher for Airbnb Plus hosts, hosts in Italy, or for listings that have a super strict cancellation policy. This fee is calculated from the booking subtotal (the nightly rate plus cleaning fee and additional guest fee, if applicable, but excluding Airbnb fees and taxes) and is automatically deducted from the host payout. To review the service fee charged for a booking:

- o Visit your Airbnb "Transaction history" at www.airbnb.com/users/transaction_history.
- o Select a reservation that you'd like to check.
- o Click on the reservation number.
- o Under the host payout details, you'll find the Airbnb service fee.

- **Guest service fee:** This fee is typically under 14.2% of the booking subtotal (the nightly rate plus cleaning fee and additional guest fee, if applicable, but excluding Airbnb fees and taxes). The fee varies based on a variety of booking factors and is displayed to guests during checkout before they book a reservation. Guests booking a listing located in Mainland China do not need to pay a guest service fee.

<u>Important</u>: If Airbnb is required to collect VAT, the service fee and VAT amounts will be combined on the checkout page, which could make the service fee appear to be higher.

2. Host-only fee: The host-only fee structure is created so that hotels and other hospitality businesses have more control over the final price. The host-only fee ranges from 14% to 20%, plus 2% in some cases for listings with a super strict cancellation policy. It is the mandatory fee structure for many hosts, hotels, and other hospitality businesses worldwide. The fee for hosts operating listings located in Mainland China is just 10%. Software-connected property managers can often choose between a host-only fee or a shared host and guest fee by going to the Service fee tab in Payments & payouts: www.airbnb.com/account-settings/payments/pro-host-service-fee.

How do you know what fees Airbnb is charging your guests?

1. **Use the price calculator in your calendar:** When opening a specific date range in your calendar, you'll see a tab called "Open price calculator." Open it to see the price charged to guests for your selected dates or the payout to you as a host for the selected dates.

2. **Guest search:** When opening your listing details in Airbnb, you'll see a tab called "Preview listing." When opening this tab, you'll see the listing from the front end. Select a date range and see how much guests will be charged when booking your listing.

How much is your property worth on Airbnb?

Unfortunately, there is no simple answer to this question. There are a lot of things to take into consideration when estimating your potential earnings on Airbnb. Some of the most important factors are:

- **Location:** A listing in Manhattan will generally have higher earnings than a listing in a remote area.
- **Capacity:** The more guests can stay at your property, the more you can charge on Airbnb.
- **Seasonality:** Is your listing located in a ski resort in the Swiss Alps with five months of snow per year or Barcelona's city

center? The seasonality in your area has an important impact on travelers' demand, and therefore, your potential earnings.

- **Availability:** How many days per year is your property available? Do local restrictions or laws allow you to rent your property as a short-term rental 365 days per year?

- **Property quality:** The more services and amenities you offer, the more your property is worth on Airbnb. Especially if you provide some of the most popular amenities or facilities to your guests, such as a pool or parking space, you could increase your rates.

- **Airbnb listing quality.** Is your Airbnb listing 100% completed? Do you have professional photos and great reviews? Having an excellent listing profile increases the chances of getting booked and will perhaps allow you to increase your rates.

Estimated Airbnb earnings calculator

Use the estimated Airbnb earnings calculator to better understand the monthly earnings potential for an Airbnb listing in your area. You can find the tool via this link: www.airbnb.com/host/homes. To see your potential monthly earnings, open the link, and select:

- Your property location
- Your property type
- And the number of guests that can stay at your property

This Airbnb earnings calculator estimate assumes that an average listing has 15 nights booked per month at the forecasted daily prices. The forecasted daily prices are based on average prices for similar listings with a similar location, listing type, and guest capacity. How much you make may vary due to your pricing, property type, property location, actual occupancy rate, season, demand, local laws, and other factors. For example, in our business, we have some listings that generate about 2 to 4 times the estimated Airbnb earnings, mainly due to the higher occupancy and higher average nightly rates.

Availability

Smartly optimizing your listing availability will help you increase your earnings on Airbnb. This section will show you how to take advantage of the Airbnb availability settings to optimize your listing performance.

Reservation preferences

To find the "Reservation preferences" section in Airbnb, log in to your Airbnb account on a computer, select "Manage listing(s)," open your listing, click on "Availability," and scroll down to the "Reservation preferences" section.

In the "Reservation preferences" section, you set up what date and time before check-in guests can book, how much time you'll need to prepare your property, and how far in advance guests can book your property.

Advance Notice

To avoid last-minute surprise bookings, set how much notice you need before a guest arrives. Airbnb will automatically block the days in your calendar accordingly. These are your options:

- Same day arrival (with cut-off time)
- At least one day arrival notice
- At least two days arrival notice

- At least three days arrival notice
- At least seven days arrival notice

If possible, it is highly recommendable to accept same-day reservations up to the latest possible time of check-in as this will increase your last-minute bookings. We frequently get same-day reservations for our Airbnb listings. For instance, guests staying in another Airbnb that is dirty or unsafe, or guests with last-minute flight cancellations. Also, on a last-minute basis, we sometimes have Airbnb customer service representatives reaching out to us, to relocate Airbnb guests to our properties for various reasons.

If you can only accept same-day instant bookings up to a specific time, choose until what exact time guests can book. Once this time has passed, guests will only be able to send you a reservation request.

Preparation time

If you can't prepare your property for same-day check-ins, Airbnb allows you to block 1 or 2 nights before and after each reservation. This might be a lifesaver for you, but not for your earnings. Take into consideration that every day that your property is blocked, is a missed opportunity to rent it out. There could be plenty of reasons for you not to accept same-day bookings; however, many hosts say it is because of the cleaning. In our case, we offer villas with up to 8-bedrooms that can host same-day check-ins and check-outs. To make this possible, we schedule the check-in and check-outs carefully, and the properties have efficient cleaning crews. If possible, find yourself a solution to accept same-day check-in and check-outs.

Availability window

Airbnb allows you to set your listings' availability window for:

- All future dates
- 12 months in advance
- 9 months in advance
- 6 months in advance
- 3 months in advance
- Dates unavailable by default

From a commercial perspective, it is highly recommendable to select all future dates. This should have a positive effect on your ranking, visibility, and earnings. We sometimes even get reservations for almost two years in advance (Christmas, New Year's Eve, etc.) Receiving bookings will help your listing rank higher, have more visibility, and, therefore, get even more bookings. It is a visual circle.

Important note: Do you allow guests to book your listing for all future dates? It is essential that your rates are always up to date and that your listing calendar is available for or up to two years in advance. Suppose you can't ensure the accuracy of your calendar for 12 months or longer. In that case, I'd recommend choosing one of the other future availability options by accepting bookings that are not that far out.

Trip details

> *To find the "Trip details" section in Airbnb, log in to your Airbnb account on a computer, select "Manage listing(s)," open your listing, click on "Availability," and scroll down to the "Trip details" section.*

In the "Trip details" section, you can set your length of stay restrictions. Optimized length of stay restrictions will help you increase your Airbnb earnings.

Trip length

As an Airbnb host, you can decide the minimum and the maximum length of stay for your listings. These are your options:

Minimum length of stay

When it comes to setting your minimum length of stay policy on Airbnb, there are a handful of theories on the best practice to employ. Some hosts work with a three-day minimum stay policy. Others prefer week-long (or even month-long) stays. And many others allow one-night minimum stays. Depending on your market and hosting style, having the right minimum length of stay policy can tremendously boost your earnings.

The key to a successful minimum length of stay policy is being proactive and adjusting your policy by market demand, seasonality, upcoming events, and existing reservations. When implemented the right way, you can expect a significant increase in monthly earnings. Here's how to use the minimum night stay feature to your advantage:

- **Know your market:** Talk to other hosts, search on Airbnb, perhaps use short-term rental data companies such as AirDNA to learn about your market demand, supply, and trends. For example, is your destination primarily a quick-stop transit destination? Or are guests more likely to come for an entire week or month?

- **Use a longer minimum length of stay restriction for early bookings:** Protect your listing from getting one-night reservations for next month that might block that 3-week reservation from coming in.

- **Use a short- or no length of stay restriction for last-minute bookings:** Aim for longer reservations first, and when available dates get closer, release the restrictions to fill the dates.

- **Fill up the gaps:** If you receive two bookings that leave an unbooked day in between, release the length of stay restrictions for those specific dates to fill the gaps. Do this a couple of times per month, and you'll see your earnings increase significantly.

- **Update your minimum length of stay regularly:** Make the most out of your minimum length of stay settings by being proactive. Check your calendar and length of stay settings frequently to ensure that you don't miss out on opportunities such as nearby events or holidays that increase the demand.

- **Customize your minimum length of stay:** Airbnb allows hosts to customize their length of stay for certain days of the week. This can be ideal, for instance, to attract weekend reservations.

- **Select specific dates:** Take advantage of important events in your area, holidays, or any other reason to have a longer minimum length of stay restriction by updating the "Additional requirements" tab. Select the required dates and insert the minimum length of stay.

Maximum length of stay

If you want to maximize your Airbnb earnings, then allowing guests to stay for whatever length of stay in your property could be a great way to increase earnings. However, sometimes this won't be possible:

- **Local regulations:** In some places, local laws won't allow you to rent longer than a certain number of days, or local regulations may change the rights your guests have depending on the number of nights they stay. In some US cities, not having a maximum length of stay might cause complications, such as 28+ days tenant laws.
- **Personal usage:** When you or someone else is using the property occasionally.
- **Personal reasons:** Some hosts prefer not to have guests staying more than a certain number of days because of personal reasons. For instance, hosts that live on the property themselves are often more restrictive when it comes to

extended stays, so imagine having a complicated guest residing for six months.

When allowing an unlimited maximum length of stay, leave the Airbnb maximum stay tab open, without any number displayed.

Additional requirements

In this tab, you can select a specific length of stay restriction for certain dates. Use this tab to release your restrictions for last-minute stays or to increase your restrictions for high demanded dates.

Expert tip: For new Airbnb listings without reviews, release your last-minute minimum stay restriction entirely as this will help you get your first bookings and, therefore, the first couple of reviews much faster. Having good reviews will result in more bookings. This is a great way to make a jump start on Airbnb.

Sync calendars

To find the "Sync calendars" tab in Airbnb, log in to your Airbnb account on a computer, select "Manage listing(s)," open your listing, click on "Availability," and open the "Sync calendars" tab.

In the "Sync calendars" tab, you can import or export your Airbnb calendar to synchronize it with other calendars. This is beneficial when you list your property on several booking websites to prevent multiple guests from booking the same dates by synchronizing your Airbnb calendar with your other calendars. The most significant benefit is that your calendars will be up to date, allowing you to accept instant bookings without having to work with an external channel manager software.

Calendar importing

Calendar importing will enable you to automatically keep your Airbnb calendar up to date with an external calendar that supports the iCalendar (the standard Internet format for exchanging calendar information) format. Including Google calendar or the calendar on Booking.com, HomeAway, VRBO, and TripAdvisor. How to import a calendar:

1. Login to your Airbnb profile and select the "Calendar" tab.
2. In your calendar view, click on "Availability Settings."
3. Scroll down and click on "Import Calendar."
4. Copy the URL for your other calendar into the "Calendar Address (URL)" field.
5. Name your calendar (Tip: to identify the URL easily. Name it after the booking platform, the link is coming from).
6. Click on "Import calendar" to save all.

Important note: If you edit an external calendar that synchronizes with your calendar on Airbnb, it will take a few hours for those changes to be visible to guests viewing your listing. Also, with iCalendar, you can only sync your calendars up to one year in advance.

How to export your Airbnb calendar

Airbnb calendar exporting lets you export your Airbnb calendar to import it to an external calendar that supports the iCal format. This is how you can export your calendar in iCal format and add it to your external calendar:

1. Login to your Airbnb profile and select the "Calendar" tab.
2. In your calendar view, click on "Availability settings."
3. Scroll down and click on "Export Calendar."
4. Copy and paste the Airbnb calendar link into your external iCal applications.

Expert tip: this tool also allows you to synchronize your calendar with another Airbnb profile calendar under someone else's account. This might be an option if you are not the only hosts offering a specific listing, and you'd still like to accept instant bookings.

What are the advantages of iCalendar?

- Live availability and synchronization.
- Completely free of charge.
- Easy to setup.
- Most booking platforms work with iCalendar.
- Synchronize with your personal Google calendar.
- Prevent overbookings from happening.
- Save lots of time by not having to block out calendars on other platforms manually.

- A great way to scale your short-term rental business and get more reservations.

What are the disadvantages of iCalendar?

- Different calendar programs use different ways of controlling the update frequency for pulling in subscribed calendar information. Therefore depending on the platform, you work with, there might be a delay in iCalendar synchronization of minutes or up to a couple of hours.
- iCalendar only synchronizes availability; no rates and content are being synchronized.
- Ensure that you are connecting the correct calendars to prevent mistakes from happening. Failing to do so could lead to overbookings.

Example: Sean has an apartment listed on Airbnb, Booking.com, and HomeAway. He wants to have all these calendars synchronized and additionally linked with his Google Calendar. In that case, to fully synchronize his listing among these four calendars, he must connect each one of the listing calendars through a two-way connection (by importing and exporting each one of the calendars). See the picture below:

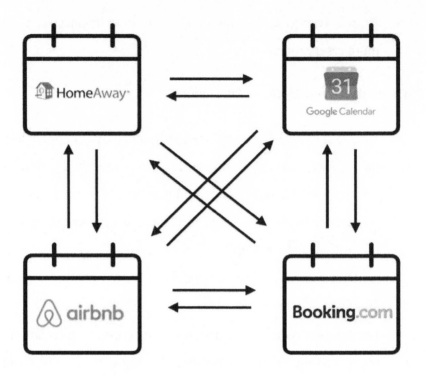

To be fully connected, Sean will have to export his iCalendars 12 times. He does this in four easy steps:

- He exports his iCalendar from Airbnb to Booking.com, Google Calendar, and HomeAway.
- He exports his iCalendar from Booking.com to Airbnb, HomeAway, and Google Calendar.
- He exports his iCalendar from HomeAway to Airbnb, Booking.com, and Google Calendar.
- He exports his iCalendar from Google Calendar to Booking.com, Airbnb, and HomeAway.

Once completed, his calendars are fully connected and are automatically synchronized.

For our business, we use iCalendar to synchronize our listings through Airbnb, Booking.com, HomeAway, and TripAdvisor, and we are delighted with the results. Our most important booking platform is Airbnb (approximately 80% of the bookings we receive). Therefore, we use other platforms mainly to fill up the gaps.

Linked Airbnb calendars

To find the "Linked Airbnb calendars" tab in Airbnb. log in to your Airbnb account on a computer, select "Manage listing(s)," open your listing, click on "Availability," and open the "Linked Airbnb calendars" tab.

If you have multiple listings on Airbnb, you can connect their calendars in the "Linked Airbnb calendars" tab. For example, you have a listing for your complete home with all bedrooms included and a cheaper listing of your home with only a couple of bedrooms available. In this case, you can link your Airbnb calendars to prevent double bookings. This is how you can link Airbnb calendars for multiple listings:

1. Go to the listings tab on Airbnb: www.airbnb.com/rooms and open one of your listings.
2. Click on "Availability."
3. Open your "Linked Airbnb calendars" tab.

4. Click on "Create linked calendars" and follow the instructions.

Important note: If one of the connected listings receives a new booking on Airbnb for a specific date, Airbnb will automatically block that same date on the corresponding calendar(s). But, if you close out a date manually on one of the connected calendars, it might not block the calendars of other listings that are connected.

Local taxes and laws

Before listing your property on Airbnb, you should educate yourself about local taxes and laws. These can often vary per country, region, property type and might change frequently. Therefore, I recommend finding professional help or a trusted local source of information to guide you through the local taxes and laws applicable to your hosting style.

Custom taxes added by you

To find the "Custom taxes added by you" tab in Airbnb, log in to your Airbnb account on a computer, select "Manage listing(s)," open your listing, click on "Local taxes and laws"' and select the "Custom taxes added by you" tab.

In the "Custom taxes added by you" tab, you can add taxes that apply to your property. Airbnb has made agreements with some governments to collect and remit local taxes on behalf of hosts. Airbnb calculates these taxes and collects them from guests at the time of booking. Airbnb then remits collected taxes to the applicable tax authority on the hosts' behalf. Here you can find a full list of governments Airbnb made an agreement with www.airbnb.com/help/article/2509/in-what-areas-is-occupancy-tax-collection-and-remittance-by-airbnb-available.

Important note: As tax laws often change, this chapter's information might be outdated or not relevant to your personal tax situation. Therefore it is recommended to get professional help and use this information as a reference. Also, if your government isn't shown in this list, then this doesn't mean that you are tax-exempt. Most governments require you to collect occupancy taxes manually.

How does occupancy tax collection and remittance by Airbnb work?

The Airbnb system determines which taxes are applicable by the address you enter for your listing. You can see these details on the "Manage your space" page. Ensure that your address is correct. Even if Airbnb automatically collects and pays certain occupancy taxes on your behalf, you may still be required to collect other occupancy taxes manually. For example, Airbnb may collect regional taxes but not local ones in some places. This is how you can check your listings for eligibility:

1. Go to "Your listings": www.airbnb.com/rooms on Airbnb and select a listing.
2. Click on "Manage listing(s)."
3. Click on "Local taxes and laws."
4. If Airbnb collects taxes for your area, you'll see a default tax collection setting on the page.

If there isn't a section for local tax collection under the "Local taxes and laws" tab, then Airbnb doesn't automatically collect and pay on your behalf for that listing. In this case, it is best to seek professional help.

How to check occupancy tax totals

You can find collected occupancy taxes listed in the gross earnings section of your Airbnb account: www.airbnb.com/users/transaction_history#gross-earnings. All guest receipts include occupancy taxes as a separate line item.

How does manual occupancy tax collection and payment work?

Most of the time, hosts need to collect occupancy taxes manually, unless automatic occupancy tax collection and payment is set up for their jurisdiction.

Collecting occupancy taxes manually

There are several ways for you to collect occupancy taxes from guests manually:

- If you're using professional hosting tools, you may be able to add taxes for a listing: www.airbnb.com/help/article/2523.
- You can include taxes within a special offer: www.airbnb.com/help/article/35.
- You can collect taxes after check-in from guests by using the Airbnb Resolution Center: www.airbnb.com/resolutions

In each scenario, you must inform guests of the exact tax amount before booking.

Important note: Only hosts that by law are required to collect occupancy taxes in person should collect them upon arrival.

Additional taxes

Airbnb allows hosts to add several different taxes and choose how to charge them. Airbnb will collect these taxes on new bookings and pay them to you. Therefore, as a host, you are responsible for submitting, paying, and reporting the correct amount to your tax authorities. How to set your additional taxes up:

1. **Choose the tax type:**
   a. Hotel tax
   b. Lodging tax
   c. Room tax
   d. Tourist tax
   e. Transient occupancy tax
   f. Sales tax
   g. VAT/GST
   h. Tourism Assessment/Fee
2. **Choose the type of charge:**
   a. Percentage per Booking
   b. Fee per guest
   c. Fee per guest, per night
   d. Fee per night
3. **Amount:** Select the tax amount in %.
4. **Add your business Tax ID:** You can find this number on your tax registration documents.

5. **Accommodations tax registration number:** This might apply only for some listings. You can find this number on your tax registration documents.

6. **Does your region provide exemptions for long-term stays?:** If this applies, select yes and insert the minimum number of days required for tax exemption.

7. **Accept the term and click on save.**

Here you can find more information about how occupancy tax collection and remittance by Airbnb works: www.airbnb.com/help/article/1036.

Your local laws

To find the "Your local laws" tab in Airbnb, log in to your Airbnb account on a computer, select "Manage listing(s)," open your listing, click on "Local taxes and laws," and open the "Your local laws" tab.

Important note: As local laws for short-term rentals often change, this chapter's information might be outdated or not relevant to your personal situation. Therefore it is recommended to get professional help and use this information as a reference.

As an Airbnb host, you need to understand the laws in your city, county, state, province, territory, and country (your "jurisdiction") that apply to Airbnb. As a platform and marketplace, Airbnb doesn't provide legal advice but gives you some practical considerations that may help you better understand your jurisdiction laws and regulations. These limitations might apply to your area:

- **Business licenses:** Many jurisdictions require owners or operators of certain businesses to apply for and obtain a permit before a company can be operating. Many local governments have sections on their websites explaining the business licensing process and provide relevant information. Contact your local jurisdiction for more information.

- **Building and housing standards:** Most local governments and jurisdictions have rules and regulations specifying minimum construction, design, and maintenance standards for buildings, including restrictions on habitability, health, and safety. Certain laws applicable to residential and non-residential uses may be relevant to your Airbnb listing. Some jurisdictions may also require an inspection of your property to make sure it meets minimum habitability standards. Contact your local government to find out what standards apply in your area and for your listing type.

- **Zoning rules**: Most cities or other local jurisdictions have laws that set out how you can use your home. These rules are often found in a zoning code, planning code, or city ordinances. You should consult these rules or regulations with your local government to see if your listing is consistent with current zoning requirements.

- **Special permit:** Some jurisdictions may require a special license to rent out your home. Contact your local government to see if you need one, and, if you do, how to get it.

- **Taxes:** Many jurisdictions require hosts to collect a tax for each overnight stay. Contact your local government to see if you need to collect any taxes.

- **Landlord-tenant laws:** When hosting extended stays, you may be subject to landlord-tenant laws that vary by jurisdiction. These may impose legal obligations on you and provide guests with certain additional legal rights. For example, in some jurisdictions, guests who stay in a home for a certain period—the exact number of days depends on jurisdiction—may establish rights as a tenant. Generally, this means that local tenancy laws could protect them, and you may not be able to remove them from your property without proceeding through the required eviction processes. Consult a local lawyer specializing in landlord-tenant law to learn more about your specific case.

- **Other rules:** It's also essential to understand and follow other regulations or rules that might apply to your listing, such as leases, timeshare ownership rules, condo board or co-op rules, homeowner's association (HOA) rules, or rules established by tenant organizations. Read your lease agreement and check with your landlord, if applicable. If you live in rent-controlled or stabilized housing, there may be special rules that apply to you. Contact your local government to ask questions about this topic.

More information about your jurisdiction's laws and regulations may be available on the Airbnb responsible hosting page: www.airbnb.com/help/article/1376 in the local regulations section. This list is not exhaustive, but it should give you a good start in understanding the laws that may apply to you. If you have questions, contact your local government, or consult a local lawyer or tax professional.

Co-hosts

Does hosting on Airbnb cost you too much time? Then working with a co-host might be the perfect solution for you. A co-host can help host your space so you can get a little support and save yourself some time.

Need help hosting your space?

To find the "Need help hosting your space" tab in Airbnb, log in to your Airbnb account on a computer, select "Manage listing(s)," open your listing, click on "Co-hosts," and select the "Need help hosting your space" tab.

In the "Need help hosting your space" tab, you can learn how co-hosts can help you manage your Airbnb. When working with a co-host, it is essential to discuss what they will and what they won't do. According to Airbnb, here are some ways co-hosts can help you:

- **Get the space guest-ready:** If a property has never been listed on Airbnb, a co-host can help you create the profile. They could also fix simple repairs, buy necessary items like towels and toilet paper, set up a lockbox, or create a house manual.
- **Create a listing:** Co-hosts could create your Airbnb listing. They could write titles and descriptions, upload photos, and help set the nightly price. For instance, you could invite me

to make me your co-host so that I can create your Airbnb listing.

- **Messaging with guests:** A co-host can message guests on your behalf, using the co-host's own Airbnb account. They can reach out to guests, answer questions, and coordinate their arrival and departure.

- **Manage reservations:** Co-hosts can manage your reservation settings and accept or decline reservation requests.

- **Welcome guests in person:** Co-hosts can greet your guests in person, give them a tour of the space, and answer questions about the house and neighborhood.

- **Help guests during their stay:** If your guests have an issue during their stay, a co-host can communicate with them and help fix the problem. For example, if a guest is locked out, their shower stops working, or their internet is down, they can call your co-host to help fix the problem.

- **Write reviews:** Co-hosts can use their personal Airbnb account to write reviews of guests on behalf of your listing. Guests will be able to review the listing and the co-host. Co-hosts can see reviews from previous guests but can't respond.

- **Update calendar and pricing:** Co-hosts can keep your listing's availability up to date and manage the listing price settings. They can also add things like seasonal pricing and weekly discounts.

- **Restock essential supplies:** Co-hosts could help stock your property with basic guest necessities like towels, toilet paper, and soap.

- **Cleaning and maintenance:** Co-hosts could clean your space themselves, work with a professional cleaning company, or both. For example, a co-host may wash towels and sheets, while a cleaning service takes care of the kitchen and bathrooms. Co-hosts could also handle general home maintenance and make sure anything that's damaged gets repaired.

- **Get help from Airbnb:** If you need to contact Airbnb to get help with a reservation or guest issue, a co-host can handle the communication and find a resolution. However, co-hosts can't open or manage Airbnb resolution center requests.

Co-hosts can't:

- **Access taxpayer information:** The listing owner's payout or taxpayer information is not accessible for co-hosts.

- **Review personal activity:** Review the listing owner's activity traveling on Airbnb as a guest.

- **See older messages:** View any messages that the host had with their guests before the co-host was added to the listing.

If needed, you can remove a co-host at any time. Additionally, guests will see your co-host(s) on your listing page, the itinerary, and all messages sent from their account.

Expert tip: Airbnb allows you to make your co-host the primary host. This way, the co-host will be shown as the main point of contact with your guests, both before and after their stay. When you choose a primary host, they'll appear as the main host on the listing, and guests will expect most interactions to be with them. This will help you save time and focus on other things, such as growing your Airbnb portfolio.

Co-host earnings

You can decide yourself how much you'd like to pay for your co-host. Most co-hosts are paid a commission on the total Airbnb earnings, and some hosts get paid a fixed fee. The fee you are paying should depend on the work/time a co-host invests in your Airbnb listing.

Setup payout routing rules

Do you want to pay your co-host a percentage of your earnings? The "Payments & Payouts Routing Rules" section in your Airbnb profile lets you split payouts into different methods of direct payouts for specific properties. Once a payout method has been verified (indicated by the Ready status), you'll have the option to split your payouts by property, percentage, or both, using routing rules. How to activate payout routing rules:

1. Visit your property section in Airbnb.
2. Click on your host profile picture.
3. Click on "Account."

4. Click on "Payment & Payouts."

5. Select "Payouts."

6. Click on "Add Payout Routing Rule."

7. Select your preferred way of directing your payouts.

Or visit: www.airbnb.com/account-settings/payments/payout-methods and continue with step 6 of the options displayed above.

Airbnb profile

To find your "Airbnb profile" tab in Airbnb, log in to your Airbnb account on a computer, select "Account," and click on the "Go to profile" tab.

Your Airbnb profile is your business card to potential guests. It shows who you are and includes information such as; personal details, listings, reviews, verifications, and more. Not to confuse with your Airbnb listing, which you create for your property. Your Airbnb profile is more about you as a person, host, or business. It is an excellent way for your audience to learn more about you before they book your property. When you have a strong profile, it will help your audience feel that you are reliable, authentic, and committed to the spirit of Airbnb. Whether you're a host or a guest, the more complete your profile is, the more reservations you're likely to receive, or the more likely another host would want to welcome you as their guest.

Most hosts don't realize that guests not only look at your listing profile; they also pay a lot of attention to your Airbnb personal profile. In fact, a study found that Airbnb Profiles have a significant impact on perceived trustworthiness for guests. Going the extra mile to create an excellent personalized Airbnb profile can boost your reservations.

Follow the instructions below to create a 100% completed and engaging Airbnb profile:

1. Upload your best profile photo:

- **Visible face:** Ensure that your face is fully visible and have a neutral or positive facial expression.
- **Smile:** Smiling helps others like you better. Plenty of studies have shown that when you smile, you appear more attractive and confident to others.
- **High-resolution:** Your photo should be high-resolution, sharp straight, and have the right color balance.
- **Brightness:** Avoid taking photos that obscure your face. Instead, ensure that the brightness of your photo is good.
- **No sunglasses:** Don't wear dark glasses or anything else that makes it look like you are trying to hide your real identity.

2. Get Verified! Finish all possible verifications, including:

- Government ID
- Phone number
- Email address
- Social Media
- Selfie

Verifying your Airbnb account will help add an extra layer of credibility and trust to your listing. This can help you stand out from other listings that don't feature any verifications. The data shows that guests are more likely to book and stay with hosts who have their profiles verified by Airbnb.

3. Create a friendly, engaging, and inviting profile description:

1. **Start with a warm introduction:** Briefly introduce yourself or your business.
2. **Tell your story:** Where are you from? Where do you live? What are you passionate about? Why are you an Airbnb host?
3. **Why should guests stay with you:** Why are you a great host? For how long have you lived in your listing's area? What insight can you offer about your local area that guests will appreciate? In what ways are you available to your guests?
4. **Conclude your description with an action point:** Thank your audience for their interest. Encourage them to book with you or reach out for any questions they might have. End your description professionally with a "thank you" note.

Expert tip: Try to keep your profile description under 125 words and ensure to write conversationally. This will make it easy for guests to read, and you'll sound more approachable and friendly. An excellent way to communicate more personally is to use contractions in your writing such as I've, we're, there's, etc.

4. Add extra information:

1. Fill out your location in the "Location tab."
2. Fill out your languages in the "Languages I speak tab."
3. Fill out your work in the "Work tab."

Airbnb profile reviews

All your Airbnb profile visitors can see your reviews from guests; these are the reviews for your listings. Additionally, your profile visitors can see all reviews from hosts for your trips that you booked with your Airbnb account. Therefore, when you use Airbnb for yourself, ensure that you collect 5-star guest reviews too.

Keep your Airbnb profile up to date

Are you changing jobs or moving to a different area? Ensure that you edit your profile to reflect these updates. You don't want any inconsistencies between what your profile says about you, and the answers you give to guests when they inquire about your property.

Conclusion on how to create the perfect Airbnb listing

It may take some effort to create an outstanding Airbnb listing, but it is absolutely worth it. You'll need to put some thought into it if you want an Airbnb Listing that will boost your reservations. Just keep in mind that all your efforts will most likely already pay off with only a single extra booking!

3. Maximize: How to increase your Airbnb earnings?

"Obtain top-ranking and outperform your competition while maximizing your Airbnb earnings."

After finding the perfect property and creating the ideal Airbnb listing, the time has come to focus on the most important opportunities that will help you increase your Airbnb earnings. In this chapter, I'll discuss your most valuable options to boost your Airbnb earnings.

Airbnb performance dashboard

To find the "Performance dashboard" in Airbnb, log in to your Airbnb account on a computer, select "Manage listing(s)," and open the "Performance" tab. Or visit: www.airbnb.com/performance/opportunities.

If you have turned on the Airbnb professional hosting tools, you can track your Airbnb performance dashboard's hosting progress. This dashboard includes historical, future, and real-time performance of your listings across business metrics or top-performing listings in your area, and the ability to compare listings against each other or similar listings in the area. Your search for improvement should start here, as there is no better way to compare your listings to the market and receive opportunities that will help you increase sales.

Opportunities

When opening the opportunities tab in your performance dashboard, you'll find a list of settings you can add to help attract more bookings and increase your ranking. Some of these settings are:

- **Offer self-check-in:** For instance, by offering a smart lock, keypad, lockbox, or 24/7 building staff.
- **Enable the flexible cancellation policy:** Select if your listing allows flexible cancellations.
- **Add cooking basics as an amenity:** Select if your listing offers cooking basics such as pots and pans, oil, salt, and pepper.
- **Allow pets at your place:** Select if your listing is suitable for pets.
- **Enable instant Book:** Select if guests can book your listing instantly.
- **Welcome guests for short stays:** Setting your minimum length of stay restriction to 1-night could reduce empty blocks on your hosting calendar.

It is highly recommended to scroll through the list and ensure that all your information is up to date. If possible, try to offer as many of the opportunities listed here. However, always think carefully if an opportunity listed here is a real opportunity for your listing. For instance, setting your minimum length of stay to 1-night or allowing pets might not be a smart option for all listings.

Quality

The quality of your Airbnb listing is measured by the number of 5-star ratings you receive from guests across the following seven categories:

- Overall quality
- Accuracy
- Check-in
- Cleanliness
- Communication
- Location
- Value

At each one of these categories, you can find the review scores, reviews, comparison to similar listings, and more. As an Airbnb host, you should read all your reviews. There is no better way to understand what guests think about their stay than by reading their reviews. The average review score on Airbnb is a whopping 4.7 out of 5 stars. Compare your review score to similar listings in your area, and try to outperform your competition by working on your guests' feedback.

Occupancy & rates

Are you curious about the performance of similar listings in your area? In the Occupancy & rates tab, you can compare your listing performance with similar listings in your area. For instance:

- The average occupancy rate
- Cancellation rate
- Length of stay
- Nightly rates

In each tab, Airbnb shows you their recommended opportunities you should work on to improve your listing's performance.

Conversion

You can review performance data across specific time frames and compare them to similar listings in the conversion dashboard. Divided into four sub-sections, it will show you different performance data points specific to your listing and comparable listings in your area:

- **Booking conversion:** The overall conversion rate is the number of bookings divided by the number of visitors who viewed your listing in the Airbnb search. The booking conversion has three stages:

- o **First-page search impression rate:** The percentage of your listing views that come from the first page of ranking search results.
- o **Search-to-listing conversion:** The percentage of clicks from guests who visited your profile in search and clicked on your listing ad to learn more.
- o **Listing-to-booking conversion:** The percentage of guests who booked your property after visiting your listing page.

- **Booking lead time:** The average booking lead time is the amount of time between the booking date and the check-in day of your reservations. Also known as the booking window.
- **Returning guests:** Returning guests are guests who have previously stayed at least once at any of your listings. To get to this percentage, Airbnb divides the total number of returning guests by the total number of all guests.
- **Views:** Here, you'll find the total listing views for your listing within a selected period.
- **Wishlist additions:** This is the average number of times your listing is added to guest wishlists.

Earnings

You'll find the total booked earnings, paid out, and expected earnings in the earning tab. You can find the stats per month or year, and learn more about the number of nights booked, unbooked nights, occupancy rate, cleaning fees, cancellation fees, and transaction history. This is a great tool to compare how your Airbnb listing's earning is developing on a yearly or monthly basis.

How to use the performance information

Knowing your statistics is the first way for you to understand where you are standing as a host and where you could be standing when improving your Airbnb business. The given statistics and opportunities in these dashboards should help you understand what to improve, to increase your earnings.

For instance, if your conversion is lower than average, then this is a potential indication that perhaps your pricing, Airbnb listing, or availability should be improved. And if your returning guests score is lower than similar listings, then perhaps you'll have to work on your guest satisfaction score or a frequent guest discount program.

I'd recommend reviewing your dashboard once a week to see where you are standing and ensure that you're taking advantage of any new opportunities Airbnb offers for your listing.

Airbnb ranking algorithm

If you want to maximize your Airbnb earnings, then having a great ranking is essential. If your guests can't find your listing because it is ranked on the last page of Airbnb search in your area, then your listing won't get booked often. The Airbnb search is somehow comparable to the Google search. The top-ranked links (listings) will receive the most views and clicks. The higher your listing ranks, the higher the number of views, clicks, and possibly bookings.

The Airbnb search ranking algorithm aims to help guests find the perfect listing for their needs and help hosts find guests who are a great fit for their space. Airbnb looks at nearly 100 different factors for every listing in every search. The exact list of features is confidential, but here are the basic categories Airbnb applies:

- **Guest needs:** Airbnb looks at the guest's factors, including where they're searching from, their previous trips, which listings they've added to their Airbnb wish list or clicked on, and more.
- **Listing details:** Airbnb considers factors such as the number of 5-star reviews, price, and listing location. It also looks at if the instant book functionality is turned on, how quickly the host of the listing responds to requests, and many other factors.
- **Trip details:** Airbnb factors in how many guests will be traveling, how long the trip will be, how far in the future the

trip is, if they have set a minimum or a maximum price, and a variety of other factors.

- **Location:** Search ranking attempts to show listings in locations that guests are most interested in booking. Airbnb found that this helps guests find a listing for their trips more efficiently and that it generates more bookings for the host community. To do this, Airbnb considers previous bookings from the guest community, and can learn where a guest will most likely book when they search a town or a city.

To understand how guests have responded to your listing in previous searches, Airbnb looks at numerous signals, but two critical factors are:

- **Clicks in search results:** When a listing is shown in search results, Airbnb considers it a good sign if a guest clicks on that listing to learn more. To ensure that this is fair for the host community, Airbnb only counts clicks from different guests.
- **Requests from a listing page.** Airbnb looks at how often guests request to book when they look at your listing. Airbnb finds that successful listings do an excellent job of helping guests decide to book.

These are some of the factors that hosts have the most control over:

- **Reviews**: The Airbnb search ranking looks at the number of completed trips, and the reviews and ratings that were left by guests. High review scores are essential to performing well in search. However, a small number of negative ratings or missed reviews from guests will not necessarily have a substantial impact on your listings' ranking.

- **Price:** Airbnb finds that price is one of the significant decision factors that guests look at when comparing listings. For that reason, it's essential to set a competitive price within your market.

- **Superhost:** The Superhost designation doesn't boost ranking. However, the factors that earn you Superhost status do.

- **New listings:** To have brand-new hosts established successfully, Airbnb ensures that new listings show up well in search rankings.

- **Response rate and response time**: Responding to requests within 24 hours helps boost your Airbnb search ranking.

- **Rejections:** The Airbnb search ranking tracks how many guests make a request to book and are denied. Occasionally, rejections are necessary, so like other factors in search ranking, Airbnb is more interested in the long-term patterns, rather than in individual rejections.

- **Instant book:** Guests on Airbnb highly value a fast and easy booking experience, and therefore are more likely to book an instant book listing than an inquiry only listing. Airbnb search aims to show listings that guests are most likely to book, and therefore boosts instant book listings in the algorithm.

Visibility in Airbnb search

Although this isn't specifically part of the search ranking, part of performing well in the Airbnb search is about being visible for guest searches. Here are some visibility factors to keep in mind:

- **Activation delay:** To give hosts time to double-check settings, generally, it takes a couple of hours for new listings to be visible in the Airbnb search.

- **Minimum and maximum nights:** If you'd like your listing to show up in the maximum number of Airbnb searches, it is essential to reduce your minimum nights stay restriction as much as possible, and similarly increase the maximum nights stay restriction.

- **Long-term stays**: To attract guests looking for stays longer than 28 days, it's recommendable to offer a monthly discount, to present a reasonable price to guests.

At the time of writing, the factors above are relevant; however, Airbnb is continuously updating the algorithm. As a result, these factors can be tested and adjusted anytime.

Unconventional ways to rank higher in Airbnb

The last chapter is based on the recommendations and information Airbnb provides on Airbnb.com about increasing the ranking for your listing. However, there are some additional, more important, and unconventional ways to rank higher in Airbnb that only few Airbnb hosts are taking advantage of:

1. **Add home safety features:** Having a safe property is a must, and Airbnb thinks about this. Ensure that your listing comes with the essential safety features such as a fire alarm, carbon monoxide alarm, fire extinguisher, emergency exit instructions, etc. Airbnb might rank your listing higher when possessing these features.

2. **A flexible cancellation policy:** Guests don't like to get charged when having to cancel their reservation. Allowing guests to cancel for free will be rewarded with a higher ranking by Airbnb, and will most likely improve your Airbnb listings' booking conversation rate. Take in mind the downsides of having a flexible cancellation policy, such as having more work, and potential revenue loss.

3. **Select as many amenities for your listing as possible:** The more amenities you select, the bigger the chances that those amenities will help guests be more attracted to your listing. Therefore, choose as many relevant amenities as possible for your listing, but only if they make sense. Example: don't offer a child-friendly apartment when children aren't allowed in the building.

4. **Increase your booking window:** If your listing isn't available, you won't get booked. Ensure that your listing has unlimited availability with the correct rates and restrictions loaded. The more availability your listing has, the higher the chances are to get booked, the higher your earnings could be, and the better your ranking will be. Example: imagine you have a guest looking for a one-year stay, but your listing has

less than one year of availability and therefore doesn't show up in this specific guest search. You just lost an opportunity to sell.

5. **Create guidebook(s):** Having guidebooks will help your guests better understand what to do when staying at your listing. Therefore, offering a guidebook will increase your ranking and likeliness to get booked.

6. **Ensure your listing is up to date:** If your listing is up to date, you are more likely to get bookings, positive reviews, and, therefore, a higher ranking.

7. **Resolve your opportunities and notifications:**

   a. Login to your Airbnb profile,

   b. Go to the menu tab and select "Manage listing(s)."

   c. Automatically your hosting "Home page" will be opened. Here, you'll find a list of opportunities and notifications to address. You can either address them or ignore them. Addressing these opportunities and notifications should result in getting more bookings. Revise carefully if it makes sense for your listing(s) to apply each of the opportunities and notifications.

                                                    ✕

Now you can temporarily offer more flexible stays

Using a Flexible cancellation policy for the next few months may help guests feel more confident booking your space

[Update your settings]

8. **Refresh your listings:** Airbnb likes you to update your listings frequently; this shows that you are an active host. I'd recommend updating your listing once every 24 hours. It might sound like a lot of work, but it isn't when doing this the smart way. Airbnb doesn't verify what precisely has been updated; they just verify if something has been updated. Therefore, you can daily:

   a. Visit your "Listing(s)" tab.

   b. Select your listing or select all your listings if you have several ones.

   c. Click on "Edit."

   d. Select the "Location" tab.

   e. Select your preferred setting.

   f. Click on save.

   g. Congrats, all your listings have been refreshed within seconds.

9. **Allow smoking, events, and pets:** As discussed before in this book, allowing events, smoking, or pets will increase your visibility in the Airbnb searches.

10. **Translate your listing into another language:** What languages do your guests speak in general? If possible, add a translation of your complete Airbnb listing in other languages. This will help increase bookings, and guest satisfaction.

11. **Add discounts:** When lowering your property's rates, it likely gets booked more often. By improving your price/quality ratio, your ranking might go up too.

12. **Add extra bedding options:** Allowing more guests to stay at your property is a great way to increase your ranking as you'll show up in more searches. Additionally, you can earn more money by charging extra guest fees, or by increasing your rates. And if you don't increase your rates, allowing more guests per reservation equals a lower rate per guest per reservation, resulting in a better price/quality and possibly higher ranking. Instead of having a sofa in the living room, you could purchase a sofa bed, or add two beds in one bedroom, etc.

13. **Wishlist's:** Guests can save properties they like and possibly are interested in, by adding them to their Airbnb wishlist. Having your listing frequently saved in Airbnb wishlists should impact your listing ranking positively. Encourage guests in your Airbnb profile to save your listing to their wishlist's.

14. **Use social media to promote your Airbnb listing:** Using social media could be a great way to generate additional traffic to your listings. Therefore, creating a Facebook or Instagram account with content about your listing and links to your Airbnb listing will help you get more views, clicks, and potential bookings. It will also help you increase your Airbnb ranking.

15. **Don't cancel bookings:** Cancelling bookings will have a negative influence on your ranking. It will also result in an Airbnb automated review on your listing, stating that you

canceled a booking. As you can imagine, this isn't very beneficial for your ranking and for having new reservations.

16. **Build trust:** Have your Airbnb profile verified by Airbnb, such as your phone number, email, social media accounts, etc. Your audience can see that you have been thoroughly verified by Airbnb, which will create confidence, resulting in more bookings, and it will possibly increase your ranking.

17. **Airbnb collections:** Ensure that your listing(s) meet the requirements to be part of some of the Airbnb collections, such as the family or business collections (you can find these collections and requirements in your listing profile under the performance tab when selecting opportunities). Being part of one of these programs results in better findability and more potential bookings. Some of the additional features are; showing up in specific search filters, a profile badge on your profile, or marketing promotion opportunities.

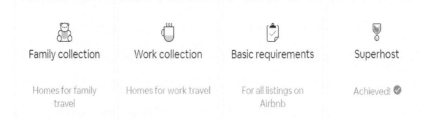

Family collection	Work collection	Basic requirements	Superhost
Homes for family travel	Homes for work travel	For all listings on Airbnb	Achieved!

Airbnb's search rank insights

The Airbnb search rank algorithm is highly secret; only a couple of Airbnb employees know the specific ranking factors and the ranking

174

value of each of these factors. Airbnb solely provides the basic ranking information mentioned in the first part of this chapter; that's all they share. When I started deep diving about Airbnb ranking, I stumbled upon this article:

https://medium.com/@childnick/hacking-airbnbs-search-rank-algorithm-8007a097382d, written by an Airbnb host from Cape Town, South Africa, who decided to start a project a couple of years ago to uncover the factors that influence search results on Airbnb. He scraped data from Airbnb using several tools; he analyzed the data and came with the following ranking factor results:

Rank	Factor	Correlation to Page Rank
1	Guest Satisfaction	0.906
2	Absolute Price	0.901
3	Listing Word Count	0.897
4	Minimum Stay Length	0.885
5	Days since calendar updated	0.884
6	Price/Bed	0.869
7	Description Length	0.867
8	Is Instant Book	0.844
9	Review Count	0.828
10	Saved to Wishlist	0.819
11	# of Amenities	0.793
12	# of Pictures	0.785
13	Is SuperHost	0.783
14	Response Speed	0.765
15	Guest Capactity	0.756
16	Hosted by Business	0.690
17	Is Business Ready	0.612
18	# of Other Properties Hosted	0.606
19	# of Beds	0.479
20	Cancellation Policy	0.379
21	Male-to-Female Ratio	0.357
22	Has Pets on Property	0.232
23	Beds per Guest	0.189
24	Account Age	0.119
25	Allows Smoking	0.087
26	"suburb name" in Description	0.047
27	"view" in Description	0.044

Most of the mentioned ranking factors align with what Airbnb has published and what most hosts have seen as essential ranking factors. I can't guarantee you the report's validity; however, please read his complete story to understand the data and collection process and then decide whether this would be an added value for your Airbnb business.

Superhost

Airbnb launched the Superhost program in 2016 to reward the most devoted hosts with a special VIP status. In short, an Airbnb Superhost is someone that goes above and beyond for their guests. Hosts who achieve Airbnb Superhost status will get benefits such as; being part of the highly used Airbnb Superhost search filter, better booking conversions, premium customer service, rewards, and, most importantly, more earnings.

How to become an Airbnb Superhost:

Every quarter, Airbnb verifies which hosts have met the Superhost criteria for the past year. If you have met the Superhost criteria, you'll earn or keep your Superhost status. These are the four Superhost requirements:

1. **Maintain a minimum of 4.8 out of 5.0 average review score:** Superhosts have a 4.8 or higher average rating based on reviews from their Airbnb guests in the past year. I'd recommend studying the "Reviews" chapter in this book carefully to ensure that you do anything you can to get great reviews.

2. **Maintain a minimum of 90% response rate:** Superhosts respond to 90% of new messages within 24 hours. Download the Airbnb app on your smartphone and activate notifications,

emails, and messages, so you are sure that you won't miss any new inquiries.

3. **Have a minimum of ten completed stays in the past year or a minimum of 100 nights booked in the last three stays:** Superhosts have completed at least 10 stays in the past 365 days or 100 nights over at least 3 completed stays.

4. **Your average cancellation rate should be lower than 1.00%.** Superhosts cancel less than 1% of the time, not including extenuating circumstances. This means 0 cancellations for hosts with fewer than 100 reservations in a year. Ensure that your calendar is always up to date; that's all you must do to achieve this requirement.

Airbnb Superhost benefits:

- **Increased visibility:** Airbnb has a special Superhost search filter for guests. This way, guests ensure that all properties shown in their search are from Airbnb Superhosts. As many guests use this filter, you'll get lots of extra visibility.

- **Increased earnings:** Research by AirDNA (an Airbnb data company) has shown that Superhosts earn up to 60% more revenue per available day.

- **Attract more guests:** Airbnb Superhosts, in general, have higher occupancy rates than regular Airbnb hosts.

- **Access to exclusive rewards:**
  o Superhosts get a 20% bonus on top of Airbnb's standard host referral bonus.

- o Once a year, Airbnb Superhosts get a bonus. They give Superhosts a choice between a $100 travel coupon, or a free professional photo session. If your Airbnb listing photos aren't perfect, you should invest this money wisely and purchase a professional photoshoot, leading to more money in the long-term. If you already have great photos, use the coupon yourself for an Airbnb stay.
- o Priority customer support; for instance, a dedicated phone line for Superhost customer service.
- o Early access to new features such as changes, updates, and more.
- o You possibly might receive Airbnb event invites.
- **You'll get a Superhost badge:** This badge will help boost your credibility as a host and will therefore result in more reservations for your listing.
- **Custom link:** A custom link for your Airbnb profile that you can personalize to be as unique as your Airbnb listing:

Becoming an Airbnb Superhost might sound like a big challenge; however, it is not that difficult. We currently have the Superhost status for over four years in a row. Just ensure to reply to all new guest inquiries within 24 hours, have your availability up to date, so you don't need to cancel any bookings, get enough stays, and ensure that you get good reviews. That's it! Find your Superhost status here: www.airbnb.com/progress/opportunities/superhost.

Airbnb Plus

The Airbnb Plus program offers a small selection of the highest quality homes, with hosts known for great reviews and attention to detail. Each Airbnb Plus home is verified through an Airbnb in-person inspection for quality and design, to ensure they have all the essentials to make you feel at home, no matter where you are in the world.

Since all listings and hosts are different, Airbnb has always had some challenges with host commitment, quality control, and standardization. The Airbnb Plus program is the perfect solution for this challenge; selecting the best properties offered by the best hosts, personally inspected by an Airbnb inspector, stunning photos taken by an Airbnb photographer, and excellent descriptions written by an Airbnb copywriter. All of this resulting in a set of somehow standardized quality listings and profiles from the best hosts in specific areas. The reward for an Airbnb Plus listing is premium placement and marketing opportunities to increase earnings. In exchange, a host needs to accept certain restrictions and commitments to Airbnb.

Within our portfolio of 100+ listings, we have a couple of Airbnb Plus listings. For some listings, being part of the program worked out positively, but for others, it didn't, and we had to take these listings out of the program. This chapter will explain how to become part of the Airbnb Plus program, the added value for your listing, and possible complications.

How to become an Airbnb Plus listing:

To be eligible for Airbnb Plus, a listing and its host must meet specific standards. The Listing should be:

- An entire place or a private room with a private bathroom.
- In a location where Airbnb Plus is available.

The Host should:

- Maintain a 4.8 average guest rating over the past year.
- Have accepted at least 95% of booking requests over the past year.
- Have not canceled any reservations (except for extenuating circumstances) over the past year.
- Maintain the Airbnb Hospitality Standards.

Airbnb Plus checklist

Does your listing meet the standards-aligned above? You can then move on to the next step and evaluate if your home meets the program's high standards. Each home that applies or gets invited to the program will be inspected with a 100+ point quality checklist. Below, you can find a recap with the most important points of the Airbnb Plus home quality checklist:

Airbnb Plus homes should have a thoughtful design

For most hosts, the checklist's biggest challenge is the design part, which is very subjective. What you think that looks beautiful and thoughtful, might be the opposite for someone else. These are the design requirements for Airbnb Plus homes:

- **Personal character:** Airbnb Plus homes should show the host's unique style and personality.

- **Welcoming in a beautiful setting**: An Airbnb Plus home should be full of character and have a one-of-a-kind feel.

- **Carefully considered design:** The central place in an Airbnb Plus space should have design features that work together to create an overall theme or style.

- **Thoughtful furniture placement:** Ensure thoughtful placement of furniture and amenities to ensure spaces don't feel cluttered.

- **Inviting:** An Airbnb Plus should feel inviting to guests.

- **Design by features:** An Airbnb Plus home should have well-crafted and elegant feature pieces that elevate the look and feel of your property.

Airbnb plus homes should be well-equipped

Airbnb Plus properties are a step above regular rentals, and so are the expectations of what hosts should provide. Some of the essential features or amenities you'll need to have at your home before being able to join the Airbnb Plus program are:

- **Reasonable WIFI speed:** As the most popular amenity on Airbnb, your Airbnb Plus home should have WIFI with download speeds of at least 5 Mbps.
- **House manual:** Airbnb Plus homes should have a printed house manual that, as a minimum requirement, includes host and emergency contact information, WIFI details, and house rules.
- **TVs:** Should come with a remote control, functional cable, or streaming capabilities.
- **Safety:** Airbnb plus homes need to have smoke and carbon monoxide detectors, a lock on the door, and a well-illuminated entryway.
- **Kitchen essentials:** Provide plates, knives, pans for cooking, salt, pepper, oil, filtered water, and a supply of tea/coffee, filters, dish soap, paper towels, etc.
- **Bedroom essentials:** A mattress that doesn't sink. Top sheet, bottom sheet, bedspread, correctly sized and matching, two pillows per guest, space to hang clothes, and a luggage rack, drawer, or shelf for guests' items.
- **Bathroom essentials:** Hot water, cold water, hairdryer, shampoo, conditioner, hand soap, body wash, toilet paper, towels, and a mirror.

- **Other essentials:** Iron and ironing board or steamer, AC or heater if needed.

Airbnb plus homes should be well-maintained

Your home must be in perfect condition when being part of the Airbnb Plus program. Therefore ensure regular maintenance. Some of the most crucial checklist points are:

- **Cleanliness:** Furniture, decor, carpet, rugs, mirrors, paint, bedding, towels, and appliances, etc., are impeccably clean, and free of stains.
- **Damages:** Furniture, decor, rugs, mirrors, paint, bedding, towels, and appliances, etc., are free of signs of wear, cracks, and damages.
- **Electrics:** Lighting, appliances, and electronics are intuitive to use and work as intended, with wires and cables being adequately organized and hidden as much as possible.
- **Aroma:** A neutral and enjoyable smell throughout. No stale odors.
- **Installation:** Fixtures, furniture, showerheads, cabin handles, etc., are adequately installed and functioning correctly.
- **Water pressure:** Water pressure should be strong. Warm and cold water should work perfectly well.
- **Outdoor areas:** Should be well-kept and free of clutter, dead plants, and excessive weeds.

- **Outdoor furniture**: Should be clean, undamaged, and fully functional.

Airbnb Plus benefits

It will take time and money for many hosts to ensure that a property is in such conditions that it is good enough to pass the Airbnb Plus checklist and standard requirements; therefore, it is essential to know what benefits Airbnb Plus could bring you. The potential benefits are:

- **Increase in earnings:** Airbnb Plus listing should get a significant increase in the number of bookings and therefore increase your earnings.
- **Built trust:** Guests will trust your listing more due to the Airbnb Plus badge on your profile.
- **Professional photography session:** You'll get an Airbnb Professional photography session for your listing.
- **Personalized Description:** You'll get a customized description written by a professional copywriter for your listing.
- **Possibly increase nightly rates**: Airbnb Plus listings are likely to charge a higher nightly rate.
- **Airbnb search benefit:** You'll be rewarded with higher Airbnb search rankings placement and will show up in the Airbnb Plus search filter.
- **Personalized design tips:** If needed, you'll get customized design tips to improve your property.

- **Premium customer support:** You'll receive priority customer support.
- **Free stuff:** You might get invited to the program, which means you won't have to pay the $149 for the inspection. Additionally, Airbnb might send you a payment for making changes in the interior design of your listing.

The possible downside of your home becoming an Airbnb Plus listing:

When reading about Airbnb Plus's benefits, becoming part of the program sounds like a great opportunity. Unfortunately, there are also some downsides to having your listing become part of the Airbnb Plus program, such as:

- **Application fee:** Luckily, we were invited and never had to pay to join the Airbnb Plus program. However, as there are already many Airbnb Plus properties in most markets, it seems that these days most hosts are being charged a $149 non-refundable application fee to cover the cost of their in-home inspection and report. Important: even if it turns out that your home is not good enough to become part of the program, Airbnb won't refund the $149 fee.
- **Photos:** All Airbnb Plus homes come with a free photography session. Your photos will be replaced with these new ones. You can't add any photos, and can't change the order. You can only take out photos or decide what photo will be the main photo for your listing. In our case, we had some Airbnb

186

Plus photographers taking photos that weren't even close to the quality of the original photos we had uploaded. Also, some Airbnb Plus photographers left out essential photos. For example, for one of our beach apartments, located right at one of the most beautiful beaches in the country, the Airbnb Plus photographer forgot to take photos of this beach, which is a lost opportunity. Airbnb photographers also tend to take mostly straight photos and don't want lights to be turned on, resulting in some spaces looking greyish and dull in the photos.

- **Descriptions:** Compared to the regular Airbnb listings, Airbnb plus listing descriptions can only have a small number of characters, making it a challenging task to describe some properties. For instance, describing one of our fully equipped 5-bedroom villas in such a short description was quite challenging. Additionally, the professional descriptions written by the Airbnb Plus copywriters were, in our case, almost always a bit vague and general, missing unique selling points and features. We, therefore, decided to overwrite most Airbnb copyrighted descriptions ourselves.

- **Investment:** If the Airbnb designers aren't happy with your listing, they'll ask you to make changes to your property before allowing you to join the program. Luckily, Airbnb provided us with a payment for making the adjustments; however, many hosts will have to pay for the changes themselves. There is a chance that you won't like the changes Airbnb wants you to make to your property. This happened to us for some of our listings, as the Airbnb Plus designer's requested changes wouldn't increase the home's look and feel, in our opinion. As we didn't think that the property would sell a lot better, we decided not to invest in making the changes and opted out of the Airbnb Plus program. On a side note, I have to say that these properties were already performing exceptionally well. Therefore, we didn't feel the urge to change a successful formula.

- **Not all Airbnb Plus listings will see increased earning:** To get back to the beach apartment example that due to the Airbnb Plus program didn't have beach photos anymore. As expected, we had a massive drop in bookings for this property and therefore decided to opt-out of the program; only a short time after we opted-in. Instantly our bookings increased again. We have had similar situations with two other properties, where the Airbnb Plus photos were just not that good as the photos we had. Those listings were also taken out of the program, after which they increased in earnings again.

- **Time:** On average, it took Airbnb Plus a couple of months from the start until the end of the Airbnb Plus registration process. It was a lengthy process that took quite some time and patience. We even had exceptional cases where it took us about a year emailing back and forth about changes and updates, before getting an Airbnb Plus property live.

- **Guest expectations:** Guests that stay in an Airbnb Plus listing have higher expectations, and therefore it is more challenging to meet those expectations and get 5-star reviews.

- **Exclusivity.** Airbnb only allows Airbnb Plus listings to be published on Airbnb and your website if you have one. Forget about publishing your listing on Booking.com, HomeAway, TripAdvisor, or any other platform, as your listing might get banned from Airbnb Plus if they find out.

If you merely look at the potential increase of earnings when joining the Airbnb Plus program, I'd recommend any host who has the essential requirements and the right property type to join the program. Give it a try and sign up; in a worst-case scenario, it might cost you some time and money. However, on the upside, there is a significant potential for extra income for Airbnb Plus properties; if you're not satisfied with the results, you can always opt-out to get your old Airbnb listing back.

Ready to apply?

Do you think your home has it all to become an Airbnb Plus property? You can sign up here: www.airbnb.com/plus.

Airbnb Luxe

In 2017, Airbnb bought full-service villa rental company Luxury Retreats. Luxury Retreats offers thousands of luxury villas in top destinations worldwide; all villas are inspected in-person and live up to the high standards. Airbnb added some Luxury Retreats villas to their portfolio, and a new Airbnb concept was born called Airbnb Luxe. A selection of thousands of exclusive homes worldwide ranging from a couple of thousand dollars weekly for a two-bedroom apartment in the Caribbean, to up to $1,000,000 a week for a private island in French Polynesia: www.airbnb.com/luxury/listing/28804753. Airbnb Luxe homes have an average nightly rate of around $2000.

What makes Airbnb Luxe unique compared to Airbnb Plus or being an Airbnb Superhost

When you book with Airbnb Luxe, you can't just select the dates and instantly confirm your reservation. Instead, you'll be connected with a dedicated trip designer who will verify at first if the chosen property is a perfect fit for your group. Once confirmed, they will help you craft a five-star stay, from the beginning until the end, including options such as private pick-up service, to securing a table at a Michelin-starred restaurant. Everything is taken care of. You'll be staying at a unique luxury home that has had a 300+ point in-person inspection, and you'll enjoy 24/7 on-trip care for any questions or inquiries you may have. The options include; vineyard estates in the

Tuscan countryside, secluded villas in Bali, or private islands in French Polynesia. Every Airbnb Luxe home is carefully vetted to ensure it's the perfect destination. To ensure complete privacy, the host profile won't be shown on the listing. Also, Airbnb doesn't publish review details as many guests and hosts of these properties, such as celebrities, business people, and politicians, highly value their privacy.

Airbnb Luxe benefits

At this time, Airbnb hasn't published any numbers about the performance of Airbnb Luxe homes. In our case, Airbnb Luxe recently reached out to us to verify if we would be interested in adding some of our listings to the program. Currently, the listings are under verification. Airbnb Luxe properties get professional photography, a professional copyrighted listing, have an Airbnb Luxe in-person inspection, verifying each listing on 300+ points, and get trip coordinators to coordinate anything guests might need. Therefore, we hope to increase earnings by having a higher occupancy rate and an increase in average nightly rates, even when considering that the commission is 25% per reservation for Airbnb Luxe properties. Airbnb Luxe is just starting in a trillion-dollar market; the opportunity is enormous.

How to qualify for Airbnb Luxe

Qualifying for Airbnb Luxe is not an easy task. Airbnb Luxe offers the world's most extraordinary homes, catering to those willing to spend. The application process is lengthy and rigorous. To qualify, your home must be exclusive, unique, pristine, and located somewhere people want to be.

To qualify for an Airbnb Luxe home, the property must pass a strict evaluation broken down into five categories:

- **Form:** Essentially, design. This represents the layout and design of the home. The Airbnb Luxe team wants homes with beautiful art, high-vaulted ceilings, and with a high level of an eye for detail, such as a closet with matching hangers. Important is what they call "socially enhancing spaces," where guests can see their group members eye to eye and have a chat together. There should be space for every guest to sit around the dining room table. There should be space for enough people in the living room to sit around and watch a movie together. Out in the gardens, there should be different seating areas for people to have a drink and chat.

- **Function:** It is all about whether things are correctly working and whether the quality standard is achieved—for instance, a fully equipped kitchen with chef quality appliances. The air conditioner and heating must be working correctly and will be tested for noise levels and efficiency. Is the pool heated? Is there an excellent bedroom to bathroom ratio? Are there extra pillows and blankets? Is there parking available?

- **Feel:** What kind of feeling does the home provide to guests? The Airbnb Luxe team will judge the architecture and style of your home. They will also evaluate the landscape and ensure its picturesque and pristine nature. Airbnb Luxe wants unique attributes; whether it's distinctive architecture, a statement-making entrance, or scenic geography, it is all about creating a unique high-end feeling.

- **Location:** Is the home somewhere where you, as a guest, would want to be, whether in the remote countryside or London's hottest neighborhood? Is the area safe and exciting? And how is the accessibility of your home?

- **Services:** Does a home have professional resources at its disposal? Daily cleaning, a chef, massages, a chauffeur, or an onsite property manager?

Airbnb's local Host Team sources homes and uses the design standard as a benchmark for initial evaluation. They then score properties against the Airbnb Luxe design rubric to ensure that all aspects of the exterior design, interior amenities, and design elements are in like-new condition. Airbnb also vets the property's technology, security, privacy, and overall accessibility. Recommended homes are then re-evaluated by a global design expert, who scores the home. After completing this process, the property is sent into the on-boarding process (including an in-person visit from a home consultant with a 300-point checklist).

Ready to apply?

Do you think your home has it all to become an Airbnb Luxe property? Then, sign up here: www.airbnb.com/luxury

Search filter opportunities

Airbnb has many different search filters that guests often use to select their preferred listings. If you'd like to maximize your property listing visibility and get more bookings, then you should take advantage of these search filters to ensure that guests can easily find you and want to book your listing. These are the most important search filters:

Traveling for work

Airbnb for work accounts for more than 15% of total Airbnb bookings. Business travelers have become an increasingly important part of Airbnb's Earnings. Therefore, it is highly recommendable to ensure that your space is "Traveling for work-ready" so that you can take advantage and increase your Airbnb earnings by hosting Airbnb guests that travel for work. Business travelers are our preferred guests. On average, they behave very professionally; they tend to stay longer than our leisure guests, rarely ask for discounts, and spend little time in the property, which keeps the costs of electricity, water, and gas relatively low.

How to become traveling for work-ready

Traveling for work?
Explore homes and boutique hotels with 5 star-ratings from business travelers

The Airbnb Travelling for work toggle

To better please guests' needs that travel for work, Airbnb has an important filter in place. When guests do a search on Airbnb for a work trip, they can select the "Traveling for work toggle" and get a list of homes and boutique hotels that are work-friendly and come with the following requirements:

"Traveling for work-friendly" homes and boutique hotels have:

- At least one business traveler review.
- High business travelers reviews (4.8+).
- A high overall review rating (4.7+).
- An indication from the host that there are a smoke alarm and a carbon monoxide alarm.
- WIFI suitable for video conferences.

Guests can further narrow their search by using the home type filter in addition to the work trip toggle.

Airbnb's Travel for Work trends

Airbnb sees some interesting trends in the way people travel for work with Airbnb:

- **Bleisure:** Combining business trips with leisure stays. Airbnb continues to see people tack on weekend days to explore the cities they're traveling to. More than 30% of Airbnb's for Work bookings include at least one weekend night.
- **Short stay business trips**: Business travelers are increasingly using Airbnb for shorter trips too, which they may have booked hotels for in the past.
- **Team travel:** Nearly 60% of Airbnb for Work trips have more than one guest. Of the 60% of Airbnb for Work trips with more than one guest, nearly 40% had three or more guests. Teams are traveling together to bond and collaborate.
- **Long-stays:** Airbnb sees extended stays and relocations being booked more than ever, ranging from long business trips or training sessions that require several weeks away to on-site projects that can last several months to a year. In the past year alone, Airbnb has seen stays with Airbnb for Work 14 days or longer grow nearly three times.

Making your listing Airbnb Travel for Work-ready is a must if you want to maximize your Airbnb earnings.

Accessibility

A great strategy to increase your Airbnb earnings is to stand out from the competition by offering additional services that make your listing more appealing for specific niches. One of these great ways to stand out is by having an accessibility friendly Airbnb home, meaning that people with disabilities can access the same things as those without a disability.

I did a quick search in one of our listing locations and saw thousands of Airbnb's. However, when selecting wheelchair-friendly accessibility features such as a wide entrance, no steps, and elevator, only 37 listings showed up. The accessibility market is a niche market, but the reward can be significant because there is little competition.

Expert tip: I'd recommend you to do an Airbnb search in your area, selecting some of the accessibility features your listing has or possibly could have, and check how many listings show up. Check the reviews and listing calendars to see if they are getting booked. Hopefully, this will help you determine whether you should prepare or offer your listing as accessibility-friendly.

Amenities

I already discussed some details about the essential amenities for your Airbnb home in the Airbnb listing chapter. Here, I'll highlight the importance of offering the right amenities to increase your earnings.

Example: An Airbnb guest that is looking for a home in your area does a search on Airbnb and selects the following popular amenities: a kitchen, washer/dryer, WIFI, TV, AC, and an iron:

If your listing doesn't have these amenities, it will not show up in this guest's search; therefore, you would have lost a potential booking.

Expert tip: The Airbnb search amenities may vary depending on your location. I'd highly recommend you verify the most important amenities in your area by running an Airbnb search as a guest. Verify what amenities guests can select in your area, and ensure that you'll add as many of these amenities (as long as they are relevant to your property). It will result in getting more bookings for your Airbnb listing.

Facilities

Do the same for the facilities. Search as a guest on Airbnb and verify the most important facilities in your area. If you have any of the listed facilities, ensure that you select them in your profile; and if you don't, consider adding some of these facilities. Perhaps, purchasing a hot tub and installing it on your private rooftop could be an excellent business decision. It might help you stand out, and will possibly allow you to increase your nightly rates and occupancy due to offering a facility that your competitors don't have.

Facilities

☐ Free parking on premises	☐ Gym
☐ Hot tub	☐ Pool

Clear all

Show 300+ stays

Facilities

☐ Free parking on premises   ☐ Gym

☑ Hot tub   ☐ Pool

Clear all   **Show 183 stays**

Expert tip: Verify how many listings in your area have a specific feature. As you can see in the example search above, there are 300+ stays that show up in this particular search, but when selecting the hot tub in the example search below, only 183 stays show up. This confirms that there are only 183 listings with a hot tub in this selected area. Properties with a hot tub have less competition, resulting in more bookings, and many guests are likely willing to pay a bit extra for having this feature. You can apply this technique to any of the search filters. It is a great way to see what your competition might not offer, and a great way to see how a search can become very narrow when selecting just a couple of requirements.

Pet friendly

House rules

☑ Pets allowed   ☐ Smoking allowed

Are pets allowed in your Airbnb property? If you want to maximize your Airbnb earnings, then it is recommendable to accept pets. Only a small percentage of Airbnb hosts allow pets. Therefore, allowing pets in your property will increase the possibility of getting booked, and you can choose to raise your rates too. For instance, by adding an extra end cleaning fee or a daily charge when bringing a pet. You can add any rules, or the fee that applies to your listing rules:

- Login to your Airbnb listing.
- Select "Manage property(s)."
- Select "Listing(s)."
- When in the listing profile, click on "Booking settings."
- Scroll down to "House rules," select" Additional rules," and write down, in short, the rules + pets fee.

All these types of amenity add-ons are great ways to increase your Airbnb earnings.

Smoking allowed

House rules

☐ Pets allowed   ☑ Smoking allowed

Should you allow guests to smoke in your listing? Considering that most Airbnb guests are nonsmokers, you should probably not allow guests to smoke inside your property. However, there's a better option. Write in your profile that smoking is permitted. Then, add to your House Rules and description that smoking is only allowed outdoors, on a balcony with the doors closed, on the terrace, or in the garden. You can now set your listing as 'smoking allowed,' which should help you capture more searches due to the smoking allowed tab that some guests will select—a great way to turn a weakness into a strength.

Important note: Be careful; some guests do not want to book listings where smoking is allowed, due to allergies, bringing kids, or simply because they don't appreciate it. Even if you have written in your description and house rules and that smoking is not allowed inside, there might be a chance that they won't read this, and therefore instantly disqualify your property. Please take in mind that, on average, guests don't read descriptions completely; they scan the text. Therefore, this might cost you some bookings too. My advice is to test with this setting to see if you notice an increase or decrease in bookings. It very much may depend on your listing, the area, type of guests, etc.

Languages

In Airbnb, guests can search listings by filtering on the host's language; this is a very convenient filter for guests who only speak their native language.

So how do you know what host languages guests in your area are looking for?

1. Got to "Airbnb.com."
2. Select "Places to stay."

3. Insert "Your home's city or area name" and click on "Search."

4. Select "More filters."

5. Scroll down to "Host language."

6. Click on "Show all." Here you see the host languages that guests can search for in your area.

×	More filters

Host language

☐ English	☐ French
☐ German	☐ Japanese
☐ Italian	☐ Russian
☐ Spanish	☐ Chinese (Simplified)
☐ Hindi	☐ Portuguese
☐ Turkish	☐ Indonesian
☐ Dutch	☐ Korean
☐ Greek	☐ Sign
☐ Hebrew	☐ Polish
☐ Danish	☐ Swedish
☐ Norwegian	☐ Finnish
☐ Czech	☐ Hungarian

Hide languages ∧

Clear all   Show 300+ stays

Suppose you, your co-host, or an employee has at least basic communication skills in one of the Airbnb search languages in your area. In that case, adding these languages will help your listing show up in more searches, increasing the likeliness of getting booked.

Additionally, you can decide to add a translation in any of the languages displayed if you feel it would make sense for your market. In our case, we offer most of our listings fully translated into Spanish and English, as 90% of our guests either speak Spanish or English. So, take that language course as you can monetize it now!

Upselling & cross-selling

If you want to maximize your Airbnb earnings, then you should apply upselling and cross-selling opportunities wherever possible. In this chapter, I'll discuss your options.

What is upselling & cross-selling on Airbnb?

Upselling on Airbnb is the practice of encouraging guests to purchase a stay at a comparable higher-end home than the one they are initially looking for, while cross-selling invites guests to buy related items or services. Though often used interchangeably, both offer distinct benefits and can be an effective strategy for your Airbnb Business to increase earnings. Upselling and cross-selling are mutually beneficial when done correctly, providing maximum value to guests while increasing earnings without many marketing channels' recurring costs. Some upselling & cross-selling opportunities are:

1. **Early check-in:** It often happens that guests are requesting an early check-in. If your home is already available, take advantage and charge your guests an early check-in fee. It is essential not to request an outrageous amount; however, you could easily ask for an extra 20% of the nightly rate for early check-ins, as most guests will find this an acceptable fee. If early check-ins happen several times a month, it could become an excellent source of extra income. To avoid overbookings, ensure that you block your calendar correctly.

I'd recommend offering this upselling technique on a last-minute basis only. This way, you can ensure that you won't get into trouble with same day check-in and check-outs.

2. **Late check-out:** For late check-outs, you could apply the same pricing strategy as for the early-check-ins. Therefore, use it to increase your earnings if it is challenging to sell your available dates between two bookings, on a last-minute basis, or in times of low demand.

3. **Minibar:** How about offering your guests some delicious local food & drink options that they can purchase for an additional fee? This is a great way to generate some extra earnings on the side. Ensure that it is clear to guests that they'll have to pay for the items. You should include a price list and billing instructions right next to the food and drinks. Upon check-out, you or your housekeeper can check if guests have used some items, restock, and if needed, submit a payment request to the guests through their reservation. Open their reservation and select the "Send or request money" tab to submit a payment request for additional services.

4. **Create packages:** Do you have guests visiting for their honeymoon, birthdays, valentine's day, or any other celebration or event? To increase your earnings and possibly your review score, you could create some package options for them. For instance, a honeymoon package that comes with flowers on the bed, a bottle of champagne, and local chocolates. You can offer these packages to guests after they

have booked, and for extra visibility, mention them in short in your description.

5. **Home upgrades:** Do you have several Airbnb listings? You could offer your guests upgrades for an extra fee. For instance, offering a property on a higher floor with better views, a king-size bed instead of queen size bed, a more spacious property, a jacuzzi, ocean view instead of pool view, etc. Offer these upgrades to your guests after they have booked. Additionally, you can increase your sales with the following trick: Add the information below to the "Things to note" description in your profile:

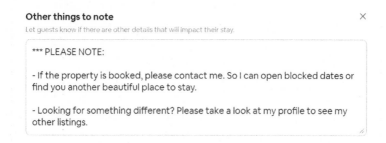

6. **Breakfast:** Offering breakfast is a great way to generate additional earnings. You can inform guests upon check-in, in a pre-trip message, or perhaps with a note inside the apartment. You can provide breakfast yourself, or use a nearby bakery or restaurant with a delivery service to deliver the breakfast and have them add your commission on top.

7. **Transportation:** Often, guests will need transportation options to get around. You could increase your earnings by taking guests around or partnering with a great local taxi driver or other transportation services. For our business, we

207

partner with a local chauffeur services company with several cars. They have all types of vehicles like regular taxis, luxury cars, minivans, and even buses. We negotiated fixed rates with the company and added our commission on top. The guest pays the transportation company, and the transportation company pays us a commission per reservation.

8. **Tours and activities:** Another excellent opportunity to earn more is to sell tours & activities. You could increase your earnings by offering guests a tour by taking them around local highlights yourself, or partner with a local tour company that pays you a commission per reservation.

9. **Restaurants and bars**: Partner with local restaurants and bars and ask if they are interested in receiving your guests in exchange for a commission fee.

10. **Airbnb Experience:** And last but not least, you could offer an Airbnb Experience. Create a unique experience and sell it to your guests and other Airbnb users in your area.

Having a successful Airbnb upselling and cross-selling strategy is all about knowing your guests. Offering additional products or services should ideally be personalized to each guests' needs. Sales messages should be well-timed, and guests should be able to see the value of what they're paying for. The boost to incremental earnings can be significant for your Airbnb business; if you take the time to understand what your guests want and carefully promote the additional products and services accordingly,

Important note: Don't underestimate your liability when offering extra services; for example, if you rent out your family's kayaks directly to your guests, you might be liable in case of an accident caused by a defect in one of your kayaks. You could cover yourself with the right insurance; however, in some cases, to not have the responsibility, it might be better to partner with a tour company that will pay you a commission. Other Example: you have an external company delivering breakfast to your guests, making it look like it comes from you. In case a guest gets food poisoned, there are chances they'll blame you for it. They might write you a bad review, and it can cause you liability issues. Think carefully about the responsibilities that come with offering extra services.

Expert tip: If you don't want to invest time in arranging activities, transportation, and other services, hire a digital assistant via platforms as www.Fiverr.com. Some digital assistants work for as low as $5 per hour, as they are based in counties with low salaries. You can put your guests in contact with your digital assistant if they like some things to be arranged and have your assistant take care of business. This way, you save time, offer a personalized service that might increase your guest satisfaction, and if you do it the right way, your earnings will increase.

Guest loyalty

Your guests are loyal when they decide to stay at your property(s) repeatedly. Depending on your location, you might have guests frequently traveling to your area. So what could you possibly do to retain guests:

- **Offer a discount:** Upon check-out, send a message to guests thanking them for their stay and offering them a 5% discount for their future stays. Explain that they can either book directly in the future and that you'll refund the 5% discount, or tell them that they can send an inquiry first so you can reply with a discounted special offer.

- **Free food & drinks:** Offer guests free services such as breakfast included for free if they decide to come back, or fill up the fridge with some local treats.

- **Free nights:** Offering free nights for extended stays are a great way to motivate guests to stay longer when returning, e.g., offering them one night for free when staying seven nights.

- **Free airport pick-up:** Do most of your guests travel by plane? Offer them a free Airport pick up service for extended stays.

- **Upgrades:** Do you have more listings on Airbnb? Offer guests a complimentary upgrade to a more upscale property.

Only few Airbnb hosts offer a guest loyalty program. In our case, renting out several properties for many years, we realized that some of our frequent guests at times stay with our competition. An easy way to see this is by reading the reviews on the guest profile; if there are host reviews from your competitors on the guest profile, you can tell that this guest has stayed with them. There could be various reasons for this: your listing not being available when the guest wanted to book, the competition having a better deal, or if guests weren't delighted with their stay and decided to shop around. As a solution, we offer discounts and free upgrades to our most important guests. They love it! We only provide this to guests that we genuinely want to host again. Our most important guest has already stayed with us over 50 times within the last three years.

Referral programs

Airbnb offers several referral programs. These are programs that allow you to earn money or credits when inviting others to join Airbnb. The Airbnb referral programs can become a very lucrative source of income for your business. For our business, we have taken advantage of our network and already produced some extra earnings.

Airbnb host referral program

This is how we earned $1980 with the Airbnb Host Referral program to date:

Referrals

Follow your friends' progress and send them tips along the way.

Carlos Cubilette
❶ Invitation expired after 0 days

Earnings

Paid out $1,980

Go to transaction history

Since your invitation has expired, this friend is no longer eligible for a referral bonus.
Refer more friends

As you can see in the screenshot above, we have generated $1980 in earnings with the Airbnb Host Referral program. It was effortless to generate these earnings. This is how we did this:

First, visit your Airbnb host referral page: www.airbnb.com/refer. You'll see how much Airbnb will pay you for every host referral on your host referral page. The payout per referral depends on your Airbnb's country and your host status. For instance, Superhosts get paid more than regular hosts for host referrals.

Airbnb gives you the option to connect your email accounts; this is how we got most referral bonuses. We connected all our email accounts and sent referral messages to all relevant contacts (thousands of contacts). The months after, we received one after another referral confirmation email. We also shared the referral link on our Social Media channels, and got several referral bonuses, earning us up to $1980 in total.

Important note: there are strict terms and conditions for referral bonuses: www.airbnb.com/help/article/1129/host-referral-program-terms-and-conditions-referring-host. For instance, the time frame your referral link is valid or the time frame the referred host has to receive their first reservation. Therefore, it might take some time before you'll receive the first referral bonuses. If you look at the time it costs you to get referral bonuses versus the potential earnings; you'll see that it is absolutely worth it. It only took us a couple of minutes of work to make $1980.

Airbnb experience host referral program

Airbnb also has a referral program for the Airbnb Experience program. This could be a great extra source of income too. In our case, if we invite someone to host an experience, we'll get $50 when they sign up and earn their first $100. In case you'd like to sign up as a first time Airbnb Experience host. You can find more information here: www.airbnb.com/refer/experiences.

Airbnb associate referral program

The Airbnb associate referral program allows you to share Airbnb stays and experiences with your guests, and earn money when they book through your link. As an Airbnb associate, you'll be paid 30% of the Airbnb guest fee every time someone books a stay through your content, and you'll be paid 25% of the Airbnb host fee every time someone books an experience through your content. You can sign up here: www.airbnb.com/associates.

Airbnb guest referral program

To invite others to use Airbnb as a guest, you can upload your email contacts on the www.airbnb.com/refer page and send them an invite or send out your referral link via social media, text messages, WhatsApp, or email. The commissions for the referral and the guests' discount might vary per host, region, or country. In our case, new Airbnb guests get $34 off their first trip, and once they complete their reservation, we get up to $23, too.

External referral programs

There are many other companies in your area that guests might be using for the first time. When having a referral program, take advantage, and use referrals to earn a commission when referring them to your guests. Some referral programs of companies that are offering their services around your listing might be:

- Transportation:
  - Uber
  - Lyft
  - Cabify
  - Mytaxi
- Food & drinks:
  - Uber Eats
  - Doordash
  - Deliveroo
  - Grubhub
- Deliver anything:
  - Glovo

214

It depends on your property's location whether the above companies offer their services in your area. Therefore, I'd recommend investigating the most popular transportation and delivery companies in your area. If they offer referrals, sign up with them so you can share your referral code or link with your guests, as this could turn into a great extra source of income.

Professional hosting tools

Knowledge is power. Airbnb has many tools and functionalities, but only few hosts know how to use all tools and functionalities the right way. If you'd like to increase your Airbnb earnings, it is essential to take advantage of any opportunity that arises. The Airbnb professional hosting tools are a great way to increase your earnings, and using them is for free (note that most of these tools are only available if you manage two or more listings). To get started, activate your professional hosting tools here:

> *To find the "Professional hosting tools" tab in Airbnb, log in to your Airbnb account on a computer and open the "Account" tab. Inside the "Account" tab, click on the "Professional hosting tools" tab and select activate.*

According to Airbnb, once activated, Airbnb will provide you with the following features and tools:

- **Multi-calendar:** The multi-calendar shows you the calendars of several of your listings on the same page. Allowing you to revise and update your rates & availability efficiently or update several listings at a time, for instance, for the following functionalities:
    - Property type
    - Fees and charges

- ○ Amenities
- ○ Location
- ○ Check-in method
- ○ House Rules
- ○ Cancellation policy
- ○ Location details
- **Hosting as a team:** As a host, you can provide individualized permissions to other team members for tasks like editing listings, setting prices, messaging guests, or accessing private information like taxpayer details.
- **Enhanced pricing and availability rules:** To support more complex rate management and give hosts greater control over how guests book, there are additional pricing and availability settings. Rates can be adjusted within the individual listing or through the multi-calendar tool. Hosts can also create and save detailed pricing and availability rulesets for different seasons or special events throughout the year.
- **On-demand performance data:** When you log-in to your Airbnb listing, you'll see a tab called Performance. The performance dashboard gives you on-demand access to performance data across multiple listings, as well as market averages. It will also surface real-time personalized tips directly within your dashboard, when available. This data helps you make strategic decisions and meet your hosting goals. You'll have access to data such as:

o **Tracking real-time and historical listing data:** The performance dashboard helps you to track and compare metrics such as market averages and listing performance across multiple listings over time. This makes identifying successful strategies easier.

o **Taking action:** The performance dashboard also shows real-time personalized tips directly, when available. This helps you to turn data into actions by making improvements to multiple listings. For example, you can create special offers for low demand dates. Airbnb says that hosts who had access to these offers have seen a 3% increase in bookings during the testing phase.

o **Time frame:** You can change the time frame of the data shown in each section by selecting a time frame. This could be historical data from the past 7, 30, or 365 days, or future data for the next 7, 30, 90, and 180 days.

o **Regions:** If you have listings in more than one region, you can choose to only show data for all regions or those you select.

o **Comparing performance data:** This graph shows how your listings perform compared to previous periods or a competitive set of listings. Toggle between the options to choose what the graph shows. When comparing periods, the graph will show the most recent period and the one before that. For example, if you selected last week, the chart will show performance for the past seven days compared to performance for the past 8 to 14 days.

- o **Comparing similar listings:** When you compare similar listings, the graph will show how your listing compares to similar listings in the area. If your listings are in multiple regions, you can increase the comparison's accuracy by filtering per region. Here you can find more information about how Airbnb chooses similar listings: www.airbnb.com/help/article/2652/how-does-airbnb-choose-which-listings-to-compare-mine-to

- **Support for standard fees:** Setting nightly rates while adding standard fees separately helps you manage your business in a way that works best for you. Adding separate costs for linens or management fees also improves accounting and visibility by highlighting payout details for each booking.

- **Pro marketing page:** Hosts with multiple listings can promote their business on Airbnb. With the pro marketing page, hosts get a unique URL, and a page where all listings are showcased on a single page. Guest reviews also appear here, demonstrating host credibility. This is how our Pro marketing page looks like:

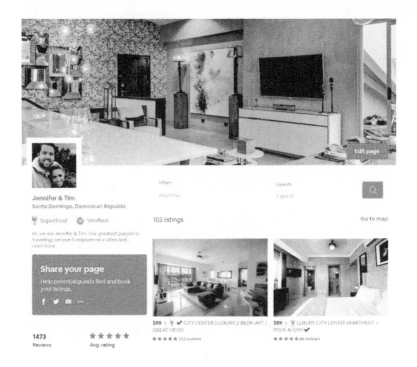

- **Integrated software partners:** To accommodate hosts who use existing software to manage their business, Airbnb has a growing network of property management software providers and channel managers. Hosts can easily connect and manage their listings on Airbnb through an integrated provider. Airbnb created a list of preferred software partners; those are the partners that support the full suite of Airbnb functionalities, and have met or exceeded technical performance benchmarks. See the full list of global partners here: www.airbnb.com/d/software-partners/

I'd recommend you invest some time in learning how to use the Airbnb professional hosting tools the right way, as this will help you in the long run save time, and improve the performance and earnings for your listing(s).

Expert tip: Whenever you see a to-do item showing in your Airbnb account, either resolve it asap or click it away by clicking on the X logo. Airbnb loves to see hosts having their listings up to date without pending items, and therefore might reward your up to date listing(s) with a higher ranking.

80/20 Rule

We run a remote Airbnb business. Our properties are based in the Caribbean while we live the largest part of the year in Spain and travel around frequently. Often, people are surprised about how we manage 100+ Airbnb properties remotely. However, it is not that complicated if you have the right processes in place. This is how we do it:

Reading 'The 4-Hour Workweek' from Tim Ferris was an eye-opener for me. This book is a step-by-step blueprint to freeing yourself from the shackles of a corporate job, creating a business to fund the lifestyle of your dreams, and living life like a millionaire, without having to be one. One of the most important lessons I learned from the book is the 80/20 rule. Also known as the Pareto Principle. This is an aphorism that asserts that 80% of outcomes or outputs result from 20% of all causes or inputs for any given event. In business, the 80/20 rule's goal could be to identify inputs that are potentially the most productive and make them a priority. For instance, once you identify factors critical to your business' success, you should mainly focus on those factors.

Applying this 80/20 rule to our Airbnb business, we realized that we had to be smarter in running our business effectively and efficiently. To get started, we first defined our goals:

- **Digital nomads:** One of our primary goals is that we want to be able to live like digital nomads, working from wherever we want to, whenever we want to. Running a complicated business with many employees is what we don't want to have. Instead, our mission is to run a remote, flexible, highly efficient, and highly profitable Airbnb business with minimized staff and low costs.

- **Secure future passive income through assets:** This is a future goal, as running an Airbnb business is not what passive income looks like. It is a lot of work, and it never stops. However, the return on investment can be significant if you do it right. Our goal is to create passive income in the long run. By the year 2030, we would like to own at least 20 properties that, eventually, when mostly paid off and rented long-term, should generate us a steady monthly rental income without having to invest that much time. To reach this goal, we decided to leverage our real estate short-term rental knowledge by increasing the ROI (return on investment). We did this by listing these properties on Airbnb; thanks to Airbnb, we more than doubled our earnings compared to what traditional long-term rentals would have brought us. Some of our properties generate a yearly Net ROI (net return on investment - the cost of investment $\times$ 100%) of up to 20%. The increased earnings allow us to invest more money in real estate and grow our portfolio faster. Our future goal is to have enough passive income to live comfortably. Currently, we are working towards achieving this goal.

To reach our goals, we decided to prioritize our time and focus on what truly makes us money:

1. **Investing in real estate:** There are almost no better ways to invest your money long-term than investing it in real estate. The market value of real estate, generally in the long-run, increases while at the same time you can obtain an income out of the rent. It is relatively easy and cheap to finance real estate, and in some countries, real estate income is lower-taxed compared to other sources of income. Therefore, we decided to invest in real estate and maximize the revenue by offering the properties as short-term rentals on Airbnb. This is easily doubling our earnings compared to long-term rental earnings. Our investment properties are our primary source of income, and we hope to grow this even further by purchasing more properties.

2. **Property management Model:** To spread risk and to leverage our network, our second most important source of income is offering short-term rentals that we advertise for the owners, charging them a commission per reservation.

3. **Rental arbitrage**: Leasing a property long-term and subletting it on Airbnb is a business model that can be very profitable for some properties. If business goes well, your earnings per property might be higher than with the property management model. However, be careful that things could

quickly go wrong. For instance, during the COVID-19 pandemic, many rental arbitrage companies went bankrupt or came into financial trouble due to their high monthly costs. We only have one property that we apply this strategy to as we could get it for a low monthly lease, allowing us to generate decent earnings with it on Airbnb.

4. **Focus on your core business:** For the listings that we manage on a commission per reservation basis, we don't offer cleaning, maintenance, key handovers, or any other services that don't bring us significant earnings. Why? Because of the 80/20 rule, it is hard to make good money on cleaning, maintenance, key handovers, etc. We'd have to hire and manage staff to offer these services, which costs time and money. Many property owners prefer not to work with us for not offering these services. However, we don't mind; we are running a highly efficient and profitable remote business, and offering these services would complicate this. Managing our Airbnb business costs us a couple of hours of work daily; still, I have time to run my digital marketing agency for short-term rental companies: www.RentalsMarketing.com. With Rentals Marketing I have done many marketing projects for property management companies, Airbnb hosts, and boutique hotels worldwide. Often I see that they face similar challenges; they try to do it all and lose focus. Often, the issue is that they offer too many extra services that do not generate sufficient income while pushing up their costs by hiring extra staff. Therefore, in our case, the 80/20 rule is a winning

225

strategy with less work generating greater profits, by solely focusing on the essential business activities that generate the highest revenue and lowest costs.

5. **Choose your marketing/sales channels carefully:** Most property management companies will try to be on any possible booking platform; they have a website, work with local travel agencies, etc. Imagine the time and money it costs to keep everything up to date! It would be much easier to find out your most important channels and fill up your place mainly using a small selection of channels, or even better, just one: Airbnb! The problem with offering your property(s) on many booking platforms is that if your bookings come from several platforms, your performance on each of these platforms will be average, your listings will never achieve top-ranking and will never get booked often on any of the platforms. When we started this business, we wanted a website and wanted to offer all listings on all possible booking platforms. So we asked ourselves, why? We already have had some issues with guests that booked directly with us and had left without paying for their reservations, damages that weren't paid for, or no-shows that left us without payment. Our average occupancy on Airbnb for our most important properties was already around 90% year-round. So why would we take so much effort only to produce a little more? We then decided not to create a website or advertise on more platforms. Instead, now we focus most of our time on Airbnb. We even ask guests that reach out directly to book

through Airbnb. Why? Because Airbnb verifies guests, offers insurance, and customer service help if needed – and it helps increase our ranking, resulting in more bookings. From our point of view, it is worth paying Airbnb's commission in exchange for their services. This strategy helped us scale our business and offer 100+ Airbnb listings at this time. We do have about 50% of our listings on other Channels like HomeAway, TripAdvisor, Booking.com, etc. But we hardly get bookings from those platforms. We use them to fill up the gaps.

When starting your Airbnb business, think carefully about your goals. Why are you doing it? What do you want to achieve? And create a plan to get to where you want to be. There is no wrong or right. The only thing that matters is that you are enjoying what you are doing while reaching your goals.

Reviews

The importance of online reviews these days goes without saying, irrespective of the industry, product, or service. As consumers, we are offered so many choices and options, which make decision-making extra challenging. And because of the infinite number of products and services out there, we place a high value on reviews and online opinions before we decide to purchase. It is comforting to know someone else tried the product before we spend our money on it, hoping for the best.

Airbnb is a community where success is partly measured by review scores. Positive reviews for your Airbnb listing result in a higher ranking and higher occupancy rate, and as a result, should help you increase earnings. On Airbnb, guests can give ratings from one to five stars on:

- **Overall experience:** Overall, how was the stay?
- **Cleanliness:** Did guests feel that the property was clean and tidy?
- **Accuracy:** How accurately did the listing page represent the space? For example, guests should be able to find up-to-date info and photos in the listing description.
- **Value:** Did the guest feel that the property provides good value for money?

- **Communication:** How well did you communicate with your guests before and during the stay? Guests often care that their host responds quickly, reliably, and frequently to their messages and questions.
- **Check-in:** How smoothly did check-in go?
- **Location:** How do guests feel about the neighborhood?
- **Amenities:** How do guests feel about the amenities that are available during their stay? Guests often care that all the amenities listed are available, effective, and in good condition.

In each category, hosts can see how often they get five-star scores from each guest. And additionally, guests can score the property with an overall rating. Visit the performance tab in your Airbnb listing profile and click on reviews to see your guest reviews.

Each review for a specific property is published on the Airbnb listing of that same property and your Airbnb profile. On your Airbnb profile, you can find all reviews for your listings and for stays booked with your account.

How to get great 5-star reviews

- **Know your property:** Receiving outstanding Airbnb reviews starts with offering a good quality product (your property). The best way to ensure your property will get good reviews is to test it yourself. Stay overnight in your property occasionally, just as a guest would do. Use anything a guest might use, ensure that everything works as it should be, check the cleanliness, check amenities, and ensure that property instructions for questions that might arise are provided.

- **Having an accurate Airbnb listing**: Will help you to set realistic expectations towards your guests. One of the most important reasons hosts don't get 5-star reviews is because they or the listing might have delivered lower expectations than expected. Therefore, keep your Airbnb listing simple and straightforward, and don't oversell expectations. Don't say your space is a 5-star property when you are not truly going to deliver on that—resulting in some of your guests being disappointed. Or don't say that there are stunning views when there's not much to see. Not meeting guest expectations will result in lower review scores.

- **Excellent host communication:** Be fast, friendly, specific, and welcoming. It is often possible to have an Airbnb space with imperfections and still get a great review score due to excellent customer service. The other way around, offering a great property but having poor communication might be a more challenging problem to overcome, as the service you provide as a host can either make or break a guest's stay.

- **Smooth check-ins and check-outs.** Most Airbnb listings don't have a 24-hour reception that can always guarantee a smooth check-in and check-out. Therefore, good communication about the check-in and check-out procedure is essential for having guests enter or leave your property most conveniently. If possible, an in-person check-in and check-out will do miracles. Upon check-in, briefly guide the guests through your property and answer any questions they might have. Upon check-out, verify how their stay was, and if satisfied, ask them to leave a review, and tell them that they will receive a 5-star review from you for being a great guest.

- **Address issues promptly and seriously:** Are you a new Airbnb host? Then I can guarantee you one thing: you'll be facing some problems during hosting, such as miscommunication with guests, rules & regulations that might not be respected, technical issues or complaints, etc. Having issues doesn't mean that guests won't give you a 5-star review after their stay. You have the matter in your own hands, as it is the way you respond to issues - do you resolve them? How much time do you take to resolve them? Do you compensate the guest if needed? We once had a guest checking-in in the middle of the night at one of our properties. Unfortunately, due to my error, I send him the wrong location. For 1.5 hours, he tried to get in, but he couldn't as we were sleeping, and no-one was available to help. After 1.5 hours, he decided to leave to find a nearby hotel. When I saw his messages the next morning, I realized I messed up. I decided to call him and explained everything to him openly. I told him about the awful mistake I made, I apologized, offered a solution, and guess what? He left a 5-star review; he even came back a couple of months later. It is all about how you respond to issues. Be understanding, kind, honest, and prompt. And after resolving the problems, confirm if the guest is satisfied, and check back with them if there is anything else that they might need.

- **Having the right price:** No one likes the feeling of paying too much. Having the right price for your listing is essential for your success on Airbnb. If your place is relatively cheap, then it is more likely to receive good reviews, as your price-quality/price perception will be better than when offering an overpriced property.

- **Read all your reviews:** Your guest feedback is worth gold. Ensure that you address issues or inconveniences pointed out by guests in their reviews. If you have received a terrible review, turn it into a positive one by replying to the guest review: thank the guest for their feedback and explain how you have addressed the issue. This way, your audience will see that you are hands-on and resolve problems when they arise. Also, when an issue is handled correctly, and your audience can read that in reply to the bad review, then you have turned a potential deal-breaker into a unique selling point - well done!

- **Encourage happy guests to write reviews:** As an experienced host, often during a guest's stay, I can already feel due to the communication with our guests, whether they are unhappy, somehow satisfied, or delighted with their stay. Whenever we think that guests enjoyed their stay, we are proactive and encourage them to leave a review. This way, we motivate guests who enjoyed their stay to write reviews (and hopefully good ones). In general, guests who are just satisfied won't leave reviews. Most of the guests that write reviews are either very happy or unhappy.

- **Surprise your guests:** Guests love being surprised! This could be anything such as giving flowers, bottled water, local treats, a welcome note, lavish bathroom amenities, a complimentary breakfast, local tips, Netflix, Disney+ or Amazon TV access, etc. Small giveaways or extras will help you improve your guest satisfaction score.

How to write a good review

It sounds so simple to write a positive review about your guests. However, many hosts find themselves struggling to come up with a brief, yet comprehensive review for their guests. Here's the thing about great positive reviews: it's okay if they're similar. There are only a couple of ways to say that a person is clean and considerate. If you want to write them the right way, then you should consider this:

1. **Make it personal:** Start with the names of your guests.
2. **How did you feel about the guests:** Explain how you felt about your guests. Example: have been great guests, very friendly, excellent communication, etc.
3. **How did they leave the space:** In what conditions did they leave your property upon check-out? For instance: spotless, perfect conditions, clean and tidy, etc.

4. **Are they recommended:** Would you recommend these guest to any hosts? For instance: they have been lovely guests; I'd highly recommend them to any host.

5. **Encourage them to come back soon:** For instance: I look forward to welcoming "Guest name" anytime soon.

6. **Free branding:** Promote your listing by adding the name of your listing to the review. This is good for SEO (search engine optimization) and might help your audience find your listing easily.

Example template guest review

I very much enjoyed hosting [GUEST NAME(S)] at [NAME OF YOUR LISTING]. Our experience was great from the beginning to the end. I'd highly recommend [GUEST NAME(S)] to any host, and I hope to have the opportunity to host [HIM/HER/THEM] again soon!

What to do when having to write a bad review

1. **Be rational; do not respond out of emotion:** When a guest leaves your place in terrible conditions, breathe first, see if you can talk to the guest, and figure out what happened before writing a bad review. Only when you are a 100% sure about what happened is when you should write the review.

2. **Be specific and honest:** Explain briefly what happened and why you didn't appreciate it.

3. **Don't welcome them back:** Explain that you prefer not to receive them back.

4. **Don't recommend them to other hosts:** You can suggest other hosts not to accept this guest to avoid similar issues.

The importance of always writing honest reviews is to protect the Airbnb host community from potential guests that might harm your property. Writing a bad review about a guest that misbehaved will help other hosts. If other hosts do the same, then you as a host would highly appreciate that too. Therefore, as a host community, we should protect our businesses and be honest about lousy guest behavior in the reviews we write.

How to delete a bad review

Airbnb is stringent when it comes to deleting reviews and only does so in exceptional situations. For example, if a guest says that your property is filthy while you say that the property is clean, Airbnb won't delete the guest review, even if you could prove it is clean. Why? Because it is the guest's opinion; what might be dirty for them might be clean for you. However, Airbnb has a policy with subjects that aren't allowed to be mentioned in reviews, and will delete a review when reported and found as violating the Airbnb Review policy as aligned below:

Reviews should not violate Airbnb's content policy

- Content created solely to advertise other commercial content, including company logos, links, or company names.

- Spam, unwanted content, or content that is shared repeatedly in a disruptive manner.

- Content that promotes illegal or harmful activity, that is sexually explicit, violent, graphic, threatening, or harassing.

- Discriminatory content.

- Attempts to impersonate another person, account, or entity, including a representative of Airbnb.

- Content that is illegal or violates another person's or entity's rights, including intellectual property rights and privacy rights.

- Content that includes another person's private information, including content that is enough to identify a listing's location.

Reviews should be unbiased

- Reviews are most helpful when they provide unbiased information.

- Airbnb doesn't allow individuals or entities who own or are affiliated with a listing or experience to post reviews of their business, nor does Airbnb allow individuals who are confirmed to offer competing listings or experiences to post reviews of their direct competitors.

- Guests or hosts are not allowed to provide an incentive for positive reviews, use the threat of a negative review to manipulate the desired outcome, or influence someone else to write another's review with the promise of compensation.
- Hosts are also not allowed to accept fake reservations in exchange for a positive review, use a second account to leave yourself a review, or coordinate with business partners to get positive reviews.

Reviews should be relevant

- Airbnb reviews should not include a person's social, political, or religious views.
- They can't have profanity, name-calling, and assumptions about a person's character or personality.
- It isn't allowed to add content that refers to circumstances entirely outside of another's control.
- It isn't allowed to write about services not related to Airbnb (ex. an airline, rideshare, restaurant, etc.)
- It isn't allowed to write about past Airbnb reservations, hosts, or guests, or about the Airbnb product when it does not relate to the listing, host, or guest you are rating.

How to report a review that violates this policy

To report a review for violating Airbnb's review policy, contact Airbnb via the www.airbnb.com/help/contact-us/topic page.

Expert tip: Imagine you have a guest who had some issues during their stay, and they already wrote a review right after check-out about their stay. If you expect the review to be a negative review that might harm your profile, then don't write your part of the review instantly. Reviews will only be published either after both the guest and host submitted their part of the review, or 14 days after check-out. On your listing profile, reviews show up mixed. Not in order of time, so you won't have to be afraid that this potentially harmful review will show up on top as the latest review for your listing. But on your Airbnb profile page, all reviews are being shown in timeline order from new to old. The good thing is that only the ten most recent reviews are displayed on your Airbnb profile's first page. The solution: Try to get ten other positive reviews before this review is automatically published (14 days after check-out). If you succeed in adding ten other reviews first, your bad review will automatically move to your reviews' second page. Only few guests visit this page. Especially for hosts with multiple listings, this technique is a simple but effective strategy.

Review statistics

A great way to measure your guest satisfaction score is to check your review statistics. You can find them here:
www.airbnb.com/performance/quality/overall.

In this section of your Airbnb profile, you can compare your quality ratings to similar listings in your area and read all review scores and details shared by guests. I'd recommend visiting this page weekly.

Ensure to read each one of your guest reviews and reply to them if needed. Additionally, you can compare your quality ratings to similar listings in your area. Try to outperform your competition by addressing all relevant guest feedback and optimizing your guest experience on an ongoing basis. Positively reviewed properties generate more earnings on Airbnb.

Crisis management

The first months of the COVID-19 pandemic had almost completely halted global travel. Airbnb cancellations and a massive decrease in demand hurt hosts tremendously, with many struggling to figure out what to do. As difficult as it was, as a host, these are the times you'll need to prepare your Airbnb business for. In this chapter, I'll discuss how you can prepare your business for the unexpected, and how to take advantage of a prompt changing market.

How to survive a crisis?

How to protect your Airbnb Business from a potential loss in earnings:

1. **Flexibility:** One of the most critical lessons for Airbnb businesses during a crisis is about flexibility. How flexible is your Airbnb business to survive a vast decrease in earnings for months? How can you maintain your costs as low as possible? Many Airbnb businesses came into trouble during the COVID-19 pandemic, especially businesses built on the arbitrage model, putting the owners at substantial financial risk due to their obligation to pay the monthly rent and have high fixed costs, or hosts that purchased real estate with expensive loans. The winning business model in a crisis where demand drops is the property management model; it is a 'no cure no pay' system. If there are no bookings, you don't

240

pay the owner(s) of the listing(s) you are managing. In our case, luckily, about 90% of our listings fall under the property management model, and our real estate is almost debt-free. This helped us keep the costs low and even run a profitable business during the COVID-19 pandemic.

2. **Costs control**: To stay competitive and survive a significant decrease in demand, it is essential to keep your costs low.

   a. **Independent contractors:** We run our Airbnb business using the 80/20 rule strategy. 20% of the work (marketing our listings) generates, on average, 80% of the earnings. For us, maintenance, key handling, managing staff, accounting, etc., costs a lot of time and generates low extra earnings. Example: marketing an Airbnb listing that generates $3000 monthly with an average of 6 bookings per month, earning a 15% commission is $450 monthly. While organizing, the cleaning might increase your earnings with $25 per reservation, times six reservations per month = $150. This is three times less. In our case, it would cost us even more time to organize cleaning than marketing a property. Therefore, we decided that we would only do the marketing for the listings we offer. And for the properties we own, and some exceptions left alone, we work with independent contractors to clean, maintain, and even co-host. As a result, we hardly need any fixed employees and therefore have low fixed costs, helping our business to stay flexible during a crisis, as we can cut costs tremendously if required.

b. **Automation:** Instead of personal key handovers, we use smart locks, we automatically share guidebooks and manuals with guests, we use messaging templates and auto-messaging for frequently asked questions, iCalendar to synchronize calendars, and we automate our business where-ever we think it is needed. This strategy helps us save time and costs.

c. **Services:** Don't sign up for multiyear services or partnerships that can cause severe financial trouble if bookings stop coming in. Ensure that each tool or service you use makes you more money than its costs while allowing you to pause or cancel whenever needed.

How to keep your earnings up when there's a massive drop in demand:

Most crises are different, but as an example, I'll use the COVID-19 pandemic. During the first months of the pandemic, we saw a drop-in demand of 90% for our listings, but we managed to keep 50% of our net earnings. This is how we did this:

1. **Knowledge is power:** During a crisis, it is essential to understand whether there is still demand and what the demand is looking for. Only if you know this, you can take

the right actions. We realized that the demand came from guests who needed extended stays as they couldn't leave the country, guests traveling to remote areas escaping the cities, and guests looking for a short break within their area.

2. **Increase your price/quality:** After analyzing our rates, competitor rates, and demand in the market, we realized quickly that with our current rates, it would be very challenging to get bookings. We decided to outperform all our competitors by offering substantially lower rates than theirs, giving discounts of up to 60%, both for short and extended reservations.

3. **Free cancellation:** During a crisis like the COVID-19 pandemic, most guests wanted flexibility, as one never knew what could happen within the next couple of days. So we temporarily switched all our cancellation policies from strict to flexible policies.

4. **Unique selling points:** During the COVID-19 pandemic, we decided to improve cleaning and disinfection in our properties. As a recognition, Airbnb emailed us an enhanced cleaning flyer. We uploaded the flyer as our second profile photo in the relevant listings; this helped us build trust and increased the number of bookings for those listings. This the flyer:

Welcome!

We want you to know that we're doing our part to help our Airbnb guests stay safe by cleaning and disinfecting frequently touched surfaces (light switches, doorknobs, cabinet handles, remotes, etc.) before you check in.

Enjoy your stay!

5. **Offer unique amenities:** During the COVID-19 pandemic, people significantly spend more time inside the Airbnb's they booked in many places worldwide. Therefore, hosts offering exciting entertainment in their properties could create a tremendous competitive advantage. During the outbreak, one of our bestselling apartments was an apartment with a

PlayStation 4, 58-inch Smart 4K TV and Amazon Fire TV, etc. We had several guests extending their reservations in this apartment simply because they enjoyed the entertainment.

6. **Extended stays:** We asked every single guest during the first months of the COVID-19 pandemic if they would be interested in extending or coming back for a discount; some guests accepted our offer, which helped us increase our earnings.

7. **Cancellation requests:** If guests would cancel far out, asking for a discount, we would instead offer them to reschedule their reservation for free to any other future date during the current or next year. Several guests agreed, which saved us on cancellations.

8. **Find alternative ways to promote your listings:** During the COVID-19 pandemic, demand for monthly stays increased, so we sent some of our listings to some local real estate agencies to see if they could bring us some business. Social media is also a great way to get extra visibility, or add your property(s) to alternative booking platforms to increase visibility and bookings.

9. **Ranking:** During the low demand times, your ranking is more important than ever. Ensure that you are doing anything you can to stay ranked on top. Only if guests see your listing, they can book it!

Applying the above helped us to stay profitable during the first months of the COVID-19 pandemic. It was a process of trial and error. Every crisis is different, but I'd like to show you that there are often solutions. In other words, protect your business by making the right choices when it comes to your strategy, cash flow, and costs. During a crisis, ensure that you do anything you can to increase your earnings. Put yourselves in the shoes of your guests, and offer what they are looking for.

4. Scale: How to scale your Airbnb business?

"Grow your Airbnb business the smart way by building a successful business model that easily scales. Having the growth and extra income you want without the extra work."

So far, in this book, I have discussed how to find and create the right Airbnb property. How to create a strong Airbnb listing, and how to increase your earnings. With an increase in earnings in most cases, extra work comes around. Therefore, in this chapter, I'll discuss how to scale your Airbnb business into an effective and efficient business, allowing you to handle a significant increase in bookings and workload while saving time without losing out on quality.

Automation

One of the best ways to scale your Airbnb business is through automation. There are a lot of daily tasks that depending on your type of business, could be automated. I have selected some of the most important solutions to challenges that Airbnb hosts are facing daily.

247

Additionally, I added some product and service recommendations to solve these challenges. The recommendations are based on factors such as popularity, review scores, and added value:

Dynamic pricing

One thing the highest-performing Airbnb hosts have in common is an effective and dynamic pricing strategy. On Airbnb, you can decide to update your pricing manually, automatically, or work with an external pricing tool. If you are willing to invest time in your pricing, you could do it manually and see great results. If you prefer not to invest the time, the Airbnb smart pricing tool might be a great solution, but it might underprice your listing (due to the conflict of interest Airbnb has, offering the best rate to a guest while filling up your space). If you prefer not to invest your time in updating your rates manually, and if you aren't satisfied with Airbnb's smart pricing tool, you should get an external pricing tool. Compared to the Airbnb smart pricing tool, the main benefit of some of the most popular tools is that they are made to increase your sales without having Airbnb's conflict of interest. If you are looking for an external pricing tool, I'd recommend using:

- **Pricelabs:** A powerful web-based revenue management & dynamic pricing software for short-term rentals that integrates with various property management systems. Pricelabs offers a 30-day free trial + $10 off the first payment when deciding to continue after the trial—interested in signing up? Visit www.pricelabs.co, and use the referral code: "dSHefy" to get the offer.

Important note: Pricelabs isn't the cheapest pricing tool on the market; however, its excellent functionalities justify the price.

Automated messaging

As a host, you'll spend a significant percentage of your time sending messages, most of the time repeating the same information, answering the same questions, etc. How would it be to automate most of your messages, reply in a smart way using artificial intelligence, and use a unified inbox to receive and send all communication? Wouldn't this save you lots of time? Airbnb allows you to create templates and send auto-messages; however, this will only help with some messages. If you run multiple listings, are published on several platforms, have several cleaners, or have very little time, using an external messaging tool might be the perfect solution for you. It will save you potentially from hiring someone to do the job for you. The idea behind the auto messaging software is to send standard templates for specific actions (check-ins, check-outs, booking confirmations, or frequently asked questions by your guests). Or send auto-messages to staff, such as cleaners. Some of these tools use artificial intelligence to read messages and know what template to send whenever needed. A great benefit is; responding automatically 24/7 to guests, even when you're sleeping. If done the right way, it will increase your guest satisfaction, save you time and money by being able to dedicate your time to something else, and improve your ranking and response rate score. If the Airbnb auto-messaging system isn't sufficient for you, I'd recommend using:

- **IGMS:** Has a powerful smart messaging tool allowing you to create templates and send automated messages from a unified inbox. IGMS offers a 30 USD discount for readers of this book when signing up via our referral link: www.igms.com/software/30-bonus?afmc=81

Import note: These tools don't send 100% of the messages. You'll still have to send some messages yourself. Also, not every guest will appreciate getting auto messages, as Airbnb is a platform where the personal touch is of significant value for most guests.

Market Research

Knowledge is power. Airbnb is improving its data-sharing tremendously; basic analytics are available at this time. However, suppose this isn't enough for you. In that case, several tools on the market can bring you more detailed information about your local market, both for Airbnb real estate investing and optimizing your Airbnb earnings. The benefits are that you can get precise details about the competition, rates, occupancy, reviews, and other statistics. I'd recommend using:

- **AirDNA Market Minder:** Market Minder tracks the daily performance and rental analytics of 10 million short-term rentals in over 80,000+ markets worldwide, displaying property-level data on an interactive map, including rates, availability, revenue, and more. Sign-up on www.airdna.co using the discount code: FORTUNE10 and get 10% off your first month of Market Minder.

Important note: Try their free trial or limited version at first to see if you like the provided information. When you need more depth, you can sign-up for the paid version.

Channel Management

Are you interested in listing your property(s) on several channels, and Airbnb's iCalendar synchronization isn't enough for your business? Then having a channel manager might be the right solution for you. A channel manager generally distributes your listing rates & availability to several booking channels, ensuring you live and up to date availability among the channels you work with, saving you lots of time and preventing overbookings from happening. I'd recommend using:

- **IGMS:** Has a powerful Channel Manager that enables you to automate all routine operations you usually perform on the largest vacation rental websites, including multi-platform synchronization and multiple accounts management. IGMS offers a 30 USD discount for readers of this book when signing up via our referral link: www.igms.com/software/30-bonus?afmc=81

Important note: If you only advertise your property on Airbnb, then there's no need for you to use channel management software.

Digital guidebooks

Airbnb has its guidebook feature, which is excellent when advertising things to do, places to visit, and other highlights around. Also, for property-related questions, you can use the Airbnb house manual. However, wouldn't it be easier to have one place where guests can find the answers to all their questions and perhaps show your guests everything they need to know with photos, videos, and affiliate links? Having one beautifully designed digital guidebook with the essential information about your home and surroundings will save you time (guests will ask fewer questions) and should increase guest satisfaction. I'd recommend using:

- **Hostfully:** Is a personalized and enhanced guest introduction to your property, bundled in a digital guidebook, and complete with detailed information about your property, amenities, and surrounding area made with text, photos, and videos. Hostfully offers readers of this book a 2-month free usage policy when signing up for any package using coupon code: S2H0U5B6 at www.hostfully.com.

Important note: It will take you some time to create the perfect guidebook. Ensure that you verify carefully what type of guidebook resolves your guests' needs best.

Key solutions

For most Airbnb hosts, key handling is one of those processes they love to get rid of. Guests often arrive at different times then expected, making it difficult to exchange keys in person, or guests might lose keys, or accidentally take them. Smart locks and key box solutions could resolve these problems.

Smart locks

A smart lock is a Wi-Fi or Bluetooth-enabled intelligent lock that allows users to lock and unlock a door by sending secure signals from a mobile application on their smartphone, computer, or tablet. Smart locks provide a new home security experience with the ability to customize who can access your home and when. You often can lock or unlock your door from anywhere with your smartphone, a code or some locks even allow you to unlock the door with your voice.

Last year we decided to switch all standard locks for our apartments to smart locks, and now about one year later, we would never want to go back. We are saving a tremendous amount of time; our staff has their access codes, we can see what time guests check-in, check-out, and when staff arrives and leaves. And the best thing is that we can control all of this from an app on our phones. I'd recommend:

- **Schlage Encode Smart Lock:** We have installed these smart locks at most of our properties and are completely satisfied with the results. The locks have never failed, and we can add and change codes through the app on our phones. There's no monthly subscription, and the locks are very user-friendly.

Lockboxes & key safes

A lockbox or key safe is an excellent solution for guests to get the keys to your property 24/7. A key lockbox is a simple storage device that, in most cases, is just the size of a phone, it often can be attached to a door handle or wall. The property keys are inside the box, and you can open the box with a unique code that you'll provide to your guests. Key lockboxes differ widely in strength, size, and dial format. For security reasons, when searching for an Airbnb lockbox or key safe, it is essential to find one that allows you to change the codes frequently, as you don't want all your guests to use the same code. I'd recommend:

- **Igloohome Smart Keybox 3:** Allows you to safely store the keys to your property in a secure, weatherproof lockbox that can be controlled with a smartphone.

Key storages

Having a smart lock or lockbox is not an option for your home? In that case, using a nearby key storage might be the perfect solution for you. Several key storage companies have placed key boxes with grocery stores, luggage storage shops, or laundry stores in cities worldwide. Perhaps there is one within your area. I'd recommend:

- **Keynest:** Offers thousands of locations worldwide where guests can pick up the keys to their Airbnb property. The user-friendly app allows hosts to easily share locations and instructions with guests about where and how to obtain the keys to their property.

Important note: when having a key solution, it might not be necessary anymore to check-in your guests in person. In this case, ensure that your guests have clear instructions on how to use the smart lock, and that you have a user manual or back-up in case any questions arise.

Other smart devices

With growing your Airbnb business, some challenges might arise. If you'd like to stay in full control and sustainably grow your business, then there are some great tools on the market to help you out:

- **Minut Monitor Noise Monitor:** Monitors noise, temperature, motion, and humidity. Use it as an alarm when your property is unoccupied.
- **Amazon Echo Dot Smart Speaker:** Play music, set alarms, connect to other smart devices such as your smart lock, request information such as the daily weather, or order your favorite food. Another great benefit is that it doesn't get that loud, making it a smart purchase as it won't be very likely to receive noise complaints from neighbors, when guests turn up the volume.
- **Arlo Smart Security Camera:** Live video streaming; WIFI supported, night vision, motion sensor, and weather resistant.

A great way to protect your home from the outside. For privacy reasons, never use cameras inside your home.

- **Honeywell Smart Thermostat:** Set minimum and maximum temperatures for guests, and control your home's temperature from your phone.

Expert tip: As mentioned before in this book, Airbnb has a page where Airbnb approved software partners are listed: www.airbnb.com/d/software-partners. These partners provide the requisite functionality and software connections that meet or exceed all of Airbnb's technical benchmarks. These software partners have invested in collaborating with Airbnb across all program initiatives. If a software partner isn't listed here, this doesn't necessarily mean you shouldn't use them. However, do investigate carefully before deciding to work with them.

Staff

When growing your Airbnb business, the quantity of work that comes with it will grow as well. Therefore, it is essential to scale your business and find standardized procedures for as many tasks as possible. Also, ensure that you work with highly qualified people that allow you to deliver quality, save you time, and increase your earnings.

In this chapter, I'll discuss the type of staff you might want to use in your Airbnb business, and how to scale a team the best way possible:

Housekeepers

Whether you're offering a basic room for guests to have a good night's sleep, or high-end accommodation, cleanliness is always of the utmost importance to your guests.

If a guest notices a couple of small things that aren't properly clean, they will likely perceive the whole place as dirty. That's a frustrating experience if you've worked hard to get the place clean. It is vital to anticipate this and present a wonderfully clean accommodation to your guests in the shortest possible time frame so that you can accept same-day check-ins and check-outs. But not only that; ideally, a housekeeper should also check your home on damages and missing items, and stock it with your guest amenities. This is how you can scale your housekeeping process:

- **Hire a professional housekeeper:** A flawlessly clean Airbnb home starts with finding someone that is willing and capable of doing the job. I have worked in several 5-star hotels and can tell you that the housekeepers who work at these hotels are the absolute best fit for Airbnb properties. In general, they have an incredible eye for detail and are well trained. They know how to work under pressure, as in most hotels, a housekeeper is supposed to spend about 20 to 30 minutes per room during guest occupancy. And after check-out, rooms get a more thorough cleaning, which might take in general around 30-60 minutes. Also, they are often used to working on a flexible schedule. If you'd like to work with a fixed housekeeper, put up an ad on job websites, posting that you are looking for a professional housekeeper with luxury hotel experience. Hopefully, this will help you find the right match.

- **Hire a professional cleaning company.** If you want to be genuinely hands-off, then outsource your cleaning and hire a professional cleaning company to do the job for you. Several platforms, such as www.tidy.com and www.hometime.io, can help you get a professional cleaner for a reasonable price for your Airbnb.

Expert tip: Use the Airbnb cleaning fee to cover the expenses of each cleaning. This is an easy way to make your pricing more attractive while covering the cleaning costs.

Technicians

With an increase in bookings comes an increase in wear and technical/maintenance issues. Therefore, you should have technicians or maintenance staff on standby, that can pass by as soon as a problem occurs. Depending on your property, you should have the contacts of a:

- **Electrician:** A specialist to assist with electricity issues, electricity sockets that are broken, or installing new lamps.
- **HVAC men**: A specialist to resolve all issues or maintenance related to your ACs or heating.
- **Plumber:** A specialist to fix clogged drains, possible leakages, or fix hot water issues.
- **Locksmith:** A specialist to fix broken locks, create key copies, and install or fix security systems like alarms.

Resolving these issues as fast as possible is essential to running a successful Airbnb business. It will keep your guests happy!

Co-hosts

Are you too busy to manage your Airbnb listing(s)? Hire an Airbnb co-host! Give your co-host access to your Airbnb profile and have them help you with a selection of the procedures that you can easily handover. You can pay a co-host directly from your payout settings, for instance, paying them a fixed percentage per reservation. A co-host is ideally someone close to you that knows your area, business, and property(s) very well. Someone that speaks the relevant languages and can be available for the largest part of the day.

Key-handling

If smart locks, key safes, or key storage boxes aren't an option for your home, and you can't do the check-ins yourself, then hire someone to handover the keys to your listing. In this case, it is essential to hire someone that is very flexible, friendly, speaks the guest's language, and can ideally guide your guest through the property upon check-in, answering all their questions.

Accountant

A good accountant can help you generate more income and help you save on taxes. Therefore, my accountant is practically my business consultant too. If you have an accounting background and a solid understanding of business finances, you might want to do your own Airbnb finances. However, if you lack experience managing the books of a business and expect to learn as you go, you should think twice. Running your accounting system incorrectly can hurt your business not only now, but also in the long-term.

Our staff strategy

When it comes to our staff strategy, we always try to stay as flexible as possible. We minimize the need to have fixed full-time employees. Thus, we have focused on creating a robust database of people we can call whenever we need them and pay them accordingly for the work that needs to be completed. Therefore, one of the benefits is that our business is very flexible, allowing us to lower costs tremendously when required. This is great for seasonality or, for instance, when a crisis like the COVID-19 pandemic hits. During the COVID-19 lockdown, we only had the essential employees on the payroll. And more importantly, this strategy allowed us to remain profitable while many property management and rental arbitrage companies went bankrupt or landed in substantial financial trouble. Take in mind that the disadvantage is that you have different people performing vital actions. Select the people you working with carefully.

Airbnb tasks

In the Airbnb tasks dashboard, hosts can set a checklist of steps and pre-defined task settings for recurring tasks such as cleaning and maintenance check-lists. Creating task-lists should help you save time in the long-run as it makes it easier to inform your staff and ensure quality control. To create a template:

- Log in to your Airbnb account on a computer, click on "Manage listing(s)" and open "Tasks."
- Inside the "Tasks" dashboard, go to "Templates" using the left-side menu.
- Click on "Create a template."
- Follow the steps by filling in information.
- The template will now show up on the Airbnb templates page and will be available for you to select when creating new tasks.

Finance

When growing your Airbnb business, your financial obligations might change too. Ensure that you are always in control of your finances. Understanding your Airbnb business numbers, such as all costs and earnings, are a must.

Tax payments

It is essential to understand local regulations and laws when it comes to your tax payments. You can try to figure this out yourself, save yourself tremendous time, and hire a tax accountant who can do this work for you and advise you on your best tax strategy and obligations. A popular option in the US is the company www.taxscouts.com.

Early payments

Would you like to improve or expand your Airbnb business, but you don't have the funds? You could go to your bank to get a loan or find an investor; however, for many hosts, this is simply not possible or beneficial. So if you need an alternative to get some quick cash, Airbnb reservation prepayment providers might be the perfect solution for your business. In general, Airbnb hosts get paid once a guest has checked-in while the guest already paid Airbnb in advance. Airbnb prepayment service providers can pay for your future reservation. This means that you'll have access to your money before the guests even checked in - a great way to get some extra income that you can use to invest in your business. A popular advanced payment service provider is:

- **Payfully:** A safe and secure way for hosts to get paid in advance for future reservations at their Airbnb property.

Important note: borrowing money costs money. Most of these companies charge you a fixed percentage depending on the amount they are prepaying you. Therefore, ensure only to use these services when you urgently need money or to invest it wisely.

Safety & security

Being an Airbnb host comes with specific responsibilities. One of the most critical responsibilities is offering a safe place to stay. This chapter will help you grow your business sustainably and safely, for your guests, employees, and stakeholders.

Home Safety

Your first step as a host is to find out about local government regulations and safety codes in your area. For example, in the United Kingdom, fire safety laws apply if someone pays to stay in a property, which means that as an Airbnb host in the United Kingdom, you are legally required to do a fire safety risk assessment and implement the right fire safety measures. Even if your local government regulations aren't strict about safety regulations, it still doesn't mean you should become complacent. If something happens and it turns out you as a host are to blame, you could get into serious trouble. Also, keep in mind that Airbnb will favor Airbnb properties with a range of fire safety measures in place, and that your guests will highly appreciate it. Here are some home safety measures Airbnb recommends:

- **Kitchen:** Accidental house fires often start in the kitchen. If you provide a cooking space for guests, make sure it is as safe as possible. If feasible, install electric cooking devices. Avoid placing flammable materials (such as paper towels or dishcloths) near the stove. Provide spark devices rather than matches as they present less of a risk. Don't put toasters under wall-mounted units. Ensure that there is a fire extinguisher in a visible spot and a carbon monoxide detector (if your kitchen has fuel-burning appliances such as a stove that uses gas), as well as a fire alarm. Also, include instructions on your safety card on how to switch off the gas if needed.

- **Open fires and heaters:** If guests stay with you during cold weather, I'd recommend giving them a safety tour of your property and, if relevant, explain how to use portable heaters and open fires. Educate them about the dangers of hanging clothes to dry over the heaters or close to certain types of heaters. Also, run them through the safety procedures of lighting and stoking a fire.

- **Electrics:** Check all your electric plug-in points frequently and, if needed, replace any that are damaged. Also, inspect all appliances frequently – make sure cables are in good condition and not frayed. Provide power boards with safety switches that guests can use for their devices.

- **Smoke alarms:** Smoke alarms should be installed throughout your home. These alarms can warn guests in case of fire and are a must-have for any host.

- **Carbon monoxide alarms:** If your property uses gas or oil for cooking or heating, you need to place carbon monoxide alarms in the appropriate areas. Heat alarms can also be installed for safety. Make sure to check the batteries regularly (preferably after each check-out).

- **Fire extinguishers:** You should have at least one fire extinguisher on every level of your property. They should be placed on visible spots. You could also include a fire blanket, which is a safety device designed to extinguish small fires, consisting of a sheet of fire-retardant material.

- **Emergency contact information:** Keep a list of emergency contact numbers in a central place (for instance, stuck on the fridge, by the front door, and in your welcome letter). Never assume that showing just your contact information will be sufficient. Information to include in your safety card should be:
    o Local contact numbers for emergency medical, fire, and police services.
    o Locations of fire extinguishers and fire blankets.
    o Emergency exit routes and instructions.
    o Location of a first aid kit.
    o Several of your contact numbers (i.e., include your landline plus mobile, or your partner's phone number as well as your own).

In Airbnb you can show all your safety features under the "Things guests should know" section for your listing. You could even include a paragraph on safety at the end of your property description with important safety information.

Expert Tip: if you are uncertain how to move forward with safety measures for your home, the company www.guestready.com has a team of Airbnb experts who help hosts worldwide with fire safety assessments and install relevant devices to ensure homes meet the legal requirements.

Safety for children

Do you allow kids to stay at your property? In this case, it is essential to take some extra precautions for their safety. Safe Kids Worldwide: www.safekids.org, a global organization dedicated to preventing child injuries, provides an array of resources on child safety on its website. This includes a series of simple tips:

www.safekids.org/safetytips/field_venues/home on how to make a home safer for children.

Host protection

To protect you as a host from lawsuits when things go wrong or damages by guests occur, Airbnb, in addition to the security deposit, offers host protection insurance and host guarantee. Here I'll highlight the details:

Airbnb host protection insurance

All Airbnb hosts protect liability insurance of up to $1,000,000 to protect against third-party claims for personal injury or property damage.

What's covered

The Airbnb host protection insurance program provides primary liability coverage of up to $1,000,000 per occurrence in the event of third-party claims of bodily injury or property damage.

The program covers certain property damages in common property areas outside of the listing itself (for example, a building reception). Landlords and homeowner associations are also covered in some instances. For instance, when claims are filed against them due to a guest suffering an injury during their stay or if a guest damages the building. Certain conditions, limitations, and exclusions may apply. Here are some examples of what the host protection insurance program should cover:

- A guest breaks their ankle after slipping on the rug and claims the injury against the host.
- A guest is working out in the private gym of the villa he is staying. The fitness equipment breaks, and the guest falls, causing an injury. As a result, the guest brings a claim for the injury against the host and the landlord.
- A guest accidentally drops their luggage on a third party's foot in the lobby of the building they are staying. The third-party brings a claim for the injury against the host and the landlord of the host's building.

What's not covered

The Airbnb host protection insurance program is limited to certain types of liability. Examples of things not covered include, but are not limited to:

- Property damage due to problems like pollution or mold.
- Damage or injury from something done intentionally.
- Loss of earnings.

For more information about what the Airbnb host protection insurance covers and doesn't cover, visit the Airbnb help center: www.airbnb.com/help/hosting.

Airbnb host guarantee

When you welcome guests as an Airbnb host, you count on your guests to treat your space like they would treat their own. But there are rare cases when something goes unexpectedly wrong with a stay, and if a guest is unable or unwilling to pay, the Airbnb host guarantee is intended to help.

What's covered?

The Airbnb host guarantee protects for up to $1,000,000 to Airbnb hosts for property damages, in the rare event of guest damages above the security deposit, or if no security deposit is in place. The Airbnb host guarantee is for every Airbnb host and every Airbnb listing at no additional cost. This is protected:

- Damage to a host's property (home, unit, rooms, possessions).
- Every Airbnb listing in every country.

Payments made through the host guarantee are subject to the Airbnb host guarantee terms and conditions. If damages occur, documentation (photos, receipts, etc.) will need to be provided as part of the resolution process. You can find the host guarantee terms and conditions, limitations, and exclusions here:

www.airbnb.com/terms/host_guarantee.

What's not covered?

The Airbnb Host Guarantee is limited to certain types of issues. Examples of what's not covered include, but are not limited to:

- Personal injury and property damage claims from third parties (the Airbnb host protection insurance protects those).

- Damage to shared or common areas of the building that aren't part of the listing itself.
- Cash and securities.
- Damage caused by a pet.
- Damage from ordinary wear and tear.

Certain items, including but not limited to artwork; antique items, including furniture and jewelry; valuable rugs, collectibles; and other items, may have more limited protections under the Host Guarantee. It is recommended to remove all these items from your Airbnb property, or insure them with the right insurance policy. How to submit a claim:

- Open the relevant guest reservation in Airbnb.
- Click on "Send or request money."
- Select "Request money."
- Select a reason.
- Fill out the details.

I'd recommend only proceeding with an Airbnb host guarantee claim if the claim's value is worth it. In general, you'll go through a lengthy process of several emails, which will cost you time.

Insurance

Before you list your property on Airbnb or other sites, ask yourself, what happens if all your treasured possessions are stolen? What do you do if a guest throws a house party and trashes your home? Or are you covered when a guest falls on a wet floor in your home, breaks a leg, and sues you? These things don't happen often, but they do happen. Therefore protect your property, if you'd like to grow your Airbnb business smartly. For example, see this £8,000 Banksy print that was stolen from a home rented out on Airbnb: www.standard.co.uk/news/crime/flatmates-furious-after-8000-banksy-print-stolen-after-home-was-rented-out-on-airbnb-a3171136.html.

Homeowners or renter's insurance

Most insurers don't cover those renting out a room or an entire property as a short-term business. Be careful, even if your guests behave well. If you haven't told your insurer you are renting short-term, you could be in trouble. Renting out all or a part of your property without telling your insurer could permanently invalidate your home cover even when you don't have guests staying. So before you even think about renting out your property, get the right protection in place.

Important note: The Airbnb host guarantee is not an insurance policy. If you desire additional protection, Airbnb strongly encourages hosts to purchase insurance that will cover themselves and their property for losses caused by guests if the loss is not within the terms of the host guarantee.

Liability insurance

Don't underestimate your liability. The Airbnb host protection insurance program provides primary liability coverage of up to $1,000,000 per occurrence. It sounds like a lot of money; however, this might not be sufficient depending on your property type and location. If you offer an 8-bedroom villa for 16 guests and a fire breaks out, resulting in several injured guests, then having a $1,000,000 protection is possibly on the low side. It is essential to ensure your property adequately, both for liability and to cover your belongings.

What insurance should you get

Buying cover from regular insurers can be tricky. This is because insurers class you as higher risk as they feel the chances of damage, theft, or items going missing increase. Most landlord or renter's insurance policies have a "business activity" exclusion. Landlord or renter's policies are written for landlords or renters, not business owners, and Airbnb hosts are often considered business owners. Contacting a specialist or local broker might be your best option. Therefore, I'd recommend you do the following:

- **Check if your home insurer covers you:** Call your home insurer and explain to them what you're planning to do. They may extend your existing policy for a fee or a change to your premium, get a quote, and compare it with the other options below. The price you'll be paying, and whether your insurer decides to cover you at all, will depend on whether you're letting out a spare room or a complete property, how often you'll rent it, how many people could stay there, and your previous claims history.

- **Contact a specialist broker or insurer:** The alternative option to get coverage is to contact a broker who will tailor a quote for you. You can do this if your property insurer won't extend your cover, but it's worth doing even if it will, so you can be sure you're getting the best price and cover. Companies like www.pikl.com can offer appropriate cover for Airbnb hosts.

Expanding your property portfolio

Would you like to expand your property portfolio? In this chapter, I'll discuss some good options.

Invest in real estate

Our preferred way to expand our Airbnb property portfolio is by investing in real estate. Some options to finance real estate purchases are:

- **Mortgage:** In most cases, a loan from a bank or lender helps you finance a home's purchase. When you take out a mortgage, you make a promise to repay the money you've borrowed, plus an agreed-upon interest rate.
- **Commercial mortgage loans:** A commercial mortgage is a mortgage loan secured by commercial property.
- **Specialized Airbnb Lenders:** Many lenders still hesitate to offer loans for the purchase of Airbnb real estate; therefore, working with a specialized Airbnb Lender might make this much easier for you, such as www.kramcapital.com.
- **Owner financing:** When a home buyer finances the purchase directly through the seller - instead of through a conventional mortgage lender or bank, is called owner financing. The seller acts as the lender. Instead of giving cash to the buyer, the seller extends enough credit to the buyer for the home's purchase price, minus any down payment.

- **Private financing:** Use your network or family, friends, and business partners that could lend you money.

- **Personal loans:** These are mostly taken from a bank, online lender or credit union that you pay back in fixed monthly payments, or installments, typically over two to seven years. Most personal loans aren't backed by collateral, and therefore, interest rates are often higher.

- **Investors:** Find people willing to invest as co-owners in your Airbnb properties.

- **Factoring:** This is a financial service in which the business entity sells its bill receivables to a third party at a discount to raise funds. For instance, companies like www.payfully.co can pay you upfront for your future Airbnb bookings in exchange for a commission.

Expert tip: Be cautious when financing your real estate at high-interest rates or high monthly payments. As you could get into financial trouble if you can't cover these monthly costs. Therefore, to lower the risk, we always ensure that our properties, even without Airbnb could easily cover their monthly loan payments and fixed costs when rented out long term.

Rental arbitrage

The word arbitrage is a financial term that stands for taking commodities from one marketplace and selling them for a profit in another. On Airbnb, this is when an investor rents a property from a landlord, then lists it on Airbnb and collects the difference. For instance, if you lease an apartment for $1,000 per month and rent it out on Airbnb for an average of $2,500 per month, you collect $1,500 monthly before expenses. When your expenses are around $500 monthly, your income after expenses would be $1,000 monthly. It sounds like an easy way to make money, but be careful. Unfortunately, this model has some downsides too. The COVID-19 pandemic has shown us that this business model is hazardous when having your property(s) empty, as the monthly rent is still due. During the COVID-19 pandemic, many rental arbitrage companies went bankrupt or came into financial trouble. To minimize the risk and increase your chances of success, take the following in mind while growing your rental arbitrage business:

- **Due diligence:** Before even getting started, do your due diligence exceptionally well, know your market, regulations, owner and renter rights, local laws, Airbnb laws, and financial constraints. There are huge differences between countries or areas. And you should understand all your obligations and rights.

- **Demand:** It is vital to know the demand for Airbnb properties in your area when building a rental arbitrage business. What kind of travelers visit your area? What kind of properties are they looking for? If there isn't enough demand to make a decent profit, you can get in trouble soon due to your financial obligations towards the property owner. AirDNA wrote an article about the best and worst US cities for rental arbitrage:

www.airdna.co/blog/best-worst-rental-arbitrage-airbnb-homeaway.

- **Establish startup costs:** Before getting started, determine how much money you need to launch your Airbnb rental arbitrage business. Typical start-up costs include:
  - o Application fee (credit and background check)
  - o Deposit
  - o Furnishing (can be purchased or rented)
  - o Move-in fee
  - o Filling an LLC (Limited liability Company) if necessary
  - o Legal fees

  With all these initial costs involved, it might take some time before you break even. And it is only after breaking even that you will be able to figure out the actual daily or monthly income potential.

- Rent cheap, sell expensive: It is essential to find quality properties. Lease inexpensive and rent expensive on Airbnb. Ensure that you know the demand in the market and negotiate your rent as low as possible.

- **Lower your risk:** Building a rental arbitrage business can be risky due to your financial obligations. When a crisis hits, you could get into trouble. If Airbnb gets banned in your area, you might get walloped; therefore, business interruption insurance is a good solution to minimize risk. Additionally, ensure to have enough cash flow to cover times of low demand.

- **Property acquisition:** Ready to find some properties? Take in mind that most landlords won't like the idea of having someone publish their home on Airbnb. To find the right property, you'll likely have to reach out to several property owners and be open and specific with them about your business. If you find a landlord that is ok with it, check if they have more properties that they can offer you.

- **Furniture:** To keep your investment as low as possible, it might be a good idea to lease furnished properties or lease furniture instead of purchasing it, for instance, with www.cort.com.

One of the most significant advantages of the arbitrage business model is the high-profit potential. Working with the property management model for a standard commission of 15 - 25% will, in most cases, not result in the same high earnings per property. But with the higher profit potential comes much higher financial risk. Do your due diligence carefully before getting started.

Property- management or marketing

Are you looking to start an Airbnb business without investing a cent and having low risk? Then the property management model might be your best shot. To create a successful property management business, you should have the following in mind:

- **Know the game:** Before even starting a property management company, it is essential to understand how to market Airbnb listings the right way. Property owners will hire you to either market their listings, manage them (arrange cleaning, maintenance, key handovers, etc.) or do both. Reading this book should give you enough basic knowledge to get started.

- **Choose your services:** Will you offer all kinds of services to property owners, such as cleaning, maintenance, marketing, key handling, etc., or will you specialize in some specific services such as online marketing?

- **Choose your pricing:** Most property management companies charge a commission per reservation or a fixed fee per property. Ensure that you calculate your costs carefully before offering your pricing options. Most property management companies work on a commission per reservation basis and charge between 15% - 30% depending on the services provided.

- **Acquire properties.** The biggest challenge of most property management companies is acquiring properties. Some great ways to acquire new properties are:
  - **Your network:** Talk to friends, family, and business partners and ask if they have properties that you could list, or ask if they know people with properties that are already listed on Airbnb or could be listed on Airbnb.
  - **Referral program:** Tell your friends, family, and business partners that you'll pay them a referral fee for each new property they'll bring you.

- Social media: Use social media to promote your business, post about your business looking for new properties, and try to reach out to other hosts and property owners through various social media platforms.

- Search: Search on Google, local tourism websites, Booking.com, HomeAway, and VRBO for rentals in your area and try to find the owner's contact details. If you know the name of the owner or business information, try to find their Facebook, Instagram, or LinkedIn profile and reach out.

- Airbnb guests: Always check your guests' Airbnb profiles to see if they are hosts too. If they are, ensure they enjoy their stay in your property, and once their stay is completed, reach out to them asking if they are interested in getting more reservations through your network. This way alone, we have already acquired about ten properties.

- Airbnb messaging: Reach out to a host with a nice property that has good reviews, an average looking profile, and lots of availability. Possibly this host has a quality property and no time or doesn't know how to market their listing well. Ask them through their Airbnb listing via the "Contact host" tab if they are interested in you managing their listing. However, you'll have to very cautious with this one - sending several of these messages can get your Airbnb account blocked as Airbnb sees this as spamming.

- o **Website:** Create a website for your property management business with a specific landing page to acquire new properties. You can use this landing page as a reference when reaching out to people about publishing their properties.
- o **AdWords.** Create an AdWords campaign for your property acquisition landing page, targeting people searching for property management companies in your area.

Essential success factors

- **Quality:** Would you like to grow your Airbnb portfolio? Then only offer quality properties. One lousy quality property in your portfolio might prevent you from becoming a Superhost, and might affect the performance of your other listings when getting bad reviews and bad guest experiences. Inspect all your properties in person and ensure they all meet the Airbnb quality standards.
- **Exclusivity:** Always try to get exclusivity for the properties you are publishing. This will maximize your earnings.
- **Instant book:** Always offer your properties with the instant book feature. If a property is listed somewhere else, then have your calendars synchronized and provide

the instant book feature for all your listings. It will increase your earnings.

Expert tip: Do you want to maximize your earnings as a property manager? Focus on high-end listings. It generally costs you the same effort to market a property that costs $100 per night versus a property that costs $1000 per night. When charging a fixed 15% commission per reservation, you'll have ten times higher commission earnings for a reservation in the property that costs $1000 per night.

In our business, we decided to offer a mix of different Airbnb business models. Ideally, we would only list properties we have purchased. However, as we don't want to build a pyramid of debt and not all properties are suitable as an investment property, we decided to offer the property management model to grow our business. It works great for the high-end properties that we offer, as some of them only get bookings occasionally because they are in low demanded areas or niche markets. Many people who purchase second homes don't buy them as an investment; they purchase them for themselves to use whenever they feel like it. Often people don't realize the costs that come with having a second home. As an Airbnb property manager, you can help them make money by publishing their second homes on Airbnb. About 50% of our Airbnb listings are second homes that the owners occasionally use. Additionally, we use the rental arbitrage model, but only when knowing that there is an enormous demand for a property while only paying a very inexpensive rent.

Alternative ways to get more bookings

The more properties your rental business has, the more effort it will take to get them fully booked. If Airbnb isn't bringing you sufficient bookings after applying the suggestions in this book, it is essential to think of other potential ways to get your properties booked. With this, I'll provide you some good options to increase your bookings in alternative ways:

- **Publish on other major booking platforms:** Publish your property(s) on other major booking platforms such as Booking.com, HomeAway, and TripAdvisor. Many of these companies own other booking platforms, and will automatically publish your property(s) there too. For instance, HomeAway is part of the Expedia group. If your property(s) are listed on HomeAway, there is a chance they'll publish them on Expedia and VRBO too. TripAdvisor owns, Flipkey, Niumba, and a couple of other platforms. Having your property published on TripAdvisor might result in your listings being automatically available on their other platforms too. And so does Booking.com list several of their properties on other booking platforms that are part of the same company too. Therefore, publishing your property(s) on Booking.com, TripAdvisor and HomeAway could result in your property(s) automatically being displayed on over 50 platforms all combined. Sounds great; however, remember that getting bookings from other platforms might hurt your Airbnb listing(s) performance. When getting bookings through other channels, your Airbnb listing(s) will have less availability, fewer bookings, and, therefore, a lower-ranking resulting in less visibility. As a result, we only use other platforms to fill up the gaps or to fill up various similar properties that we offer.

- **Niche platforms**: Additionally, you can create listings on smaller niche platforms used in your area, such as mid-term rental sites, sites that offer specific property types, or only target particular travelers.

- **Relocation companies:** These companies help people relocate from one country or area to another. They often need a place to stay for a couple of weeks or months. We do business with several relocation companies.

- **Airlines:** If your listings are close to an Airport, airline crew members might be staying in your area daily. You can try to get in touch with the Airlines that frequently have crew members staying in hotels or apartments in your area to see if you could host them. We often have crew members staying in some of our apartments that are located close to airports.

- **Embassies:** Embassies often have employees work for a couple of months on assignments. If your property(s) are located close to embassies, reach out, and offer your services. Note that embassies take safety and security at a very high level. Therefore, they might have a strict list of requirements for places to stay.

- **International businesses:** Do you have any large company offices in your area? Companies often send employees to other offices or countries for projects. Reach out to the office or travel managers of these companies with offices in your area to offer them your listings.

- **Hospitals:** Do you have hospitals in your area? Medical tourism might be a target market for your property(s).

- **Travel agencies:** Any travel agencies that frequently send guests to your area? Reach out to them and offer your property(s).

- **Tour operators:** Perhaps tour operators might be interested in working with you if you have plenty of availability.

- **Create a website.** Allow guests to book directly by creating a website for your property(s). This way, you could save yourself the booking platform commissions. But, you'll be fully responsible for collecting payments, liability, and guest verification if needed.

- **Social media:** Create an Instagram or Facebook account for your rentals and frequently posting about them.

- **Email marketing:** Ask guests for their email addresses and ask if you could send them promotions and specials occasionally. Email marketing is a great way to keep your guests in the loop and increase future bookings.

- **Local search engine listings:** Local search engine listings are a great way to attract guests who use search engines to find a place to stay. For example Google optimizes these listings for specific areas, but they might also display your listings with images, reviews, and more on their search page. Here are a few local search listing options:

- o Google Places
- o Yahoo! Local
- o Bing Local
- o Craigslist

- **SEO (search engine optimization):** Ensure that potential guests find your listing profiles when searching in search engines such as Google and Yahoo. To increase your website ranking focus on SEO, and create unique content that your guests might be looking for.

Applying the above should help you generate more bookings. But before doing so, it is essential to verify if you have done anything you can to optimize your earnings per opportunity before moving on trying the next thing. The 80/20 rule can be applied to this strategy too. Advertising your property(s) everywhere possible will costs you lots of time and effort, which might not even be needed if one or several platforms can bring you sufficient bookings. Apply the tips and tricks in this book and become the #1 Airbnb host in your area!

Resources

Please find below a selection of some helpful resources I have used to write this book:

Airbnb information resources:

- Airbnb News: news.airbnb.com/about-us

- Airbnb Affiliates: affiliate.withairbnb.com

- Airbnb API: airbnb.com/partner

- Airbnb Citizen: airbnbcitizen.com

- Airbnb Design: airbnb.design

- Airbnb Magazine: airbnb.com/magazine

- Airbnb Community: community.withairbnb.com

- Airbnb Night at: airbnb.com/night-at

- Airbnb Neighbors: airbnb.com/neighbors

- Airbnb Engineering: medium.com/airbnb-engineering

- Airbnb Toolkits: airbnb-toolkits.com/my_toolkits

- Airbnb Things to do: airbnb.com/things-to-do

- Airbnb YouTube: youtube.com/user/airbnb

- Airbnb Superhost: airbnb.com/superhost

- Airbnb Plus: airbnb.com/plus

- Airbnb Luxe: airbnb.com/luxury

Airbnb statistics:

- www.airdna.co

Morgan Stanley research:

- www.fullertreacymoney.com/system/data/files/PDFs/2017/
November/16th/ARCOST20171023211633_73976052-
b837-11e7-863e-cb02ae2926cb_DigitalPremium.pdf

Vacation trends:

- www.independent.co.uk/travel/instagrammability-holiday-
factor-millenials-holiday-destination-choosing-travel-social-
media-photos-a7648706.html

Airbnb safety:

- www.safekids.org

Glossary

Airbnb co-host: A person that helps an Airbnb listing owner with their space, their guests, or both.

Airbnb Experiences: An activity-centered extension of Airbnb's traditional renting business. Guests pay an individual through the platform to take part in experiences with local hosts.

Airbnb host: The noun host refers to a person who receives and entertains guests. On Airbnb, a host is a person that lists a property.

Airbnb host protection insurance: In the event someone gets hurt, or your property is damaged during a covered Airbnb stay at your place, you may be protected with Airbnb's host protection insurance.

Airbnb listing: This is a unique property page on Airbnb, with specific information about a property or space, including descriptions, photos, availability, rates, and more.

Airbnb occupancy: The formula for occupancy percentage = (the number of occupied nights) / (the total number of available nights for sale) * 100.

Airbnb Plus: An Airbnb program that allows hosts to apply to receive a "Plus" classification that recognizes listings with exceptional quality, comfort, and style.

Airbnb profile: This is a specific host and or guest page with information about a guest or host, including description, verification, and profile photo.

Airbnb Superhost: Superhosts are experienced Airbnb hosts who provide a shining example for other hosts, and extraordinary experiences for their guests. Once a host reaches Superhost status by meeting the Airbnb Superhost criteria, a badge will automatically appear on their listing and profile to help guests identify them.

Booking conversion: The average number of visitors who viewed your listing in the Airbnb search and then booked it.

Cross-selling: Selling a different product or service to an existing customer.

Digital-Nomad: Digital nomads are location-independent people that use technology to perform their job or run their businesses. Digital nomads work remotely, telecommuting rather than being physically present at a company's headquarters or office.

Guest loyalty: Is a measure of a guest's likeliness to repeat business with a company or brand.

LLC: Stands for limited liability company. This is a type of legal entity formed to own and operate a business. LLCs are very popular because they provide the same limited liability as a corporation, but are easier and cheaper to form and run.

Occupancy: The proportion of days in a month for which a property has bookings.

Outsourcing: Obtaining goods or services by contract from an outside supplier.

Property management: Property management is the overseeing of residential, commercial, or industrial real estate.

Psychological pricing: The practice of setting prices slightly lower than a whole number. An example of psychological Airbnb pricing is setting your listing price at $99 rather than $100.

Rental-arbitrage: The act of renting a property long-term, to re-rent it on a short let basis to turn a profit.

ROI: Stands for return on investment. The ROI measures the gain or loss generated on an investment relative to the amount of money invested.

Scaling: Having the ability to grow without being hampered. It requires planning, some funding, and the right systems, staff, processes, technology, and partners. As a result, you'll grow your business and the income you want while minimizing the extra work.

Search engine ranking algorithm: Search engines use algorithms to weigh varied elements to determine which webpage is most relevant to a search query.

Short-term rental: Furnished self-contained property that is rented for short periods.

Smart lock: A smart lock is an electronic and mechanical locking device that opens wirelessly with an authorized user's authentication.

Smart pricing tool: A tool to help hosts set their prices right automatically.

Target market: A particular group of consumers at which a product or service is aimed.

Upselling: A sales technique used to get someone to spend more by buying an upgraded or premium version of what's being purchased.

Final Notes

Thank you for reading How to Make a Fortune on Airbnb! I hope you enjoyed the contents of my book and received lots of value from it. If you have feedback about my work or would like to receive personalized help, please feel free to contact me by email at tim@rentalsmarketing.com; I read every email, so please do get in touch. Please visit my website: www.RentalsMarketing.com for updated content or to learn more about the services I offer. I'd be happy to get in touch!

Schedule a call

Want to get in touch for a personal coaching session? I'd love to assist. Visit my https://clarity.fm/timvernooij profile and request a call now.

Thank you!

I first want to thank you for your support and time in reading this book. Thank you to my spouse Jennifer for her support and input. She hasn't seen me much during writing this book as I spent many days at my desk. Thank you to my dad Gerard Vernooij, my uncle Huib van de Donk, and my friends Thijs de Koe, and Julia Agnes Horti for their content editing and for helping me improve the book wherever needed. Thank you to Airbnb and the community of hosts and guests for creating this unique environment where people can monetize their homes to pay for a living.

About the Author

Tim was born in 1988 and spent most of his younger years in a small city called Rhenen, located in the Netherlands. After finishing his hotel studies in Utrecht at University Tio, he worked at several high-end hotels such as the Mandarin Oriental in Barcelona, Spain, and the Intercontinental Amstel Hotel and Conservatorium Hotel in Amsterdam, the Netherlands. After meeting his spouse Jennifer, Tim decided to move to her home country, the Dominican Republic. Tim started working in the Dominican Republic at Booking.com as an Account Manager in the Caribbean region, and later as a Caribbean Vacation Rental Expert, which became his first introduction to the short-term rental industry. After a move to LinkedIn in Ireland, Tim and Jennifer decided to offer their private home on Airbnb, and it was a great success. A short time after, the couple managed to purchase several apartments. Tim quit his job at LinkedIn to become a digital nomad and travel while running their Airbnb business. The trip ended in the city of Barcelona, Spain, where they still reside. At this time, Tim is a short-term rental investor, Airbnb Superhost with 100+ listings, and founder of RentalsMarketing.com, a digital marketing agency for short-term rentals. Tim hosted thousands of guests and helped hundreds of Airbnb hosts increase earnings. Tim and Jennifer's objective is to increase their real estate investment portfolio, automatizing as much as possible to secure a future passive income.

Made in the USA
Las Vegas, NV
18 January 2022